KT-591-975

Contents

Introduction

Jake Brigance woke at 5.30 a.m. as usual, rolled out of bed, and went downstairs to make coffee for his wife, Carla.

It is just another day in the life of a small town Southern lawyer, an ambitious man with a loving wife and a new car that he has not yet paid for. But, like everyone else in Clanton, Mississippi, Jake soon hears awful news – two local men have attacked and raped ten-year-old Tonya Hailey.

After the rape Tonya's father, Carl Lee, plans his own revenge. As a result, only his lawyer and friend Jake Brigance stands between him and the electric chair. But does Jake have the experience to win this particular case? Is there a legal defense for Carl Lee's actions?

John Grisham's story takes us into the dark side of the southern United States. Clanton has a black sheriff and many good, honest citizens, but it is at times a violent place where blacks and whites have still not learned to live together. The fear and violence increases when the Ku Klux Klan become involved. They, too, want revenge.

John Grisham is the author of *The Firm, The Client,* and many other exciting titles. Grisham was born in 1955 and became a lawyer after he graduated from college. He was also involved in politics. When his first two books became bestsellers, he gave up the law profession to become a full-time writer. He now lives in Virginia and Mississippi with his wife and two children. He has sold over 55 million copies of his books and is one of the world's most popular writers.

Chapter 1   A Violent Crime

Billy Ray Cobb sat on the back of the pickup drinking a beer, watching his friend Pete Willard take his turn with the black girl. She was ten, and small for her age. She did not look at the man on top of her. He was breathing hard and swearing. He was hurting her. When he finished, he hit her in the mouth and laughed, and the other man laughed too. Then they laughed harder and rolled around the grass by the pickup, screaming like two crazy men. The girl lay in a pool of blood and beer.

Later, Willard asked what Billy Ray planned to do now that they had finished with her. Billy Ray said they should kill her.

"Are *you* going to do it?" asked Willard.

Cobb hesitated. "No, I'll let you do it."

Willard said, "It wasn't my idea. You're the one who's good at killing niggers. You do it." He thought for a minute while he finished a beer. "Let's throw her off a bridge."

"Good idea. Very good idea," said Billy Ray.

They drove past Lake Chatulla, a large, man-made mud-hole in the far southwest corner of Ford County, looking for a place to throw out their unwanted passenger. At each bridge they approached, they saw blacks fishing in the muddy water. Cobb was getting desperate by now. He turned off into a side road and stopped the pickup. They threw her into the long grass at the edge of the woods.

◆

Carl Lee Hailey did not hurry home when he got the phone call. Gwen was easily excited, and she had called him at work before when she thought the children had been kidnapped. He only became anxious when he turned into his yard and saw the police car parked next to the house.

As he opened the front door, he wondered where Tony and the boys were. Then he heard Gwen crying. To his right in the small living-room he saw a crowd around a small figure. The child was covered with towels and surrounded by crying relatives. As he went closer, the crying stopped and they moved back.

Carl Lee Hailey asked what had happened. No one answered. Only Gwen stayed by the girl, holding her hand. He knelt beside the sofa and touched the girl's shoulder. He spoke to his daughter, and she tried to smile. Both her eyes were swollen shut and bleeding.

Carl Lee stood and turned to the crowd and demanded to know what had happened.

He asked for the third time. The deputy, Willie Hastings, one of Gwen's cousins, stepped forward and told Carl Lee that some people were fishing down by the river when they saw Tonya lying in the middle of the road. She told them her daddy's name, and they brought her home.

"What happened, Willie?" Carl Lee shouted as he stared at the deputy.

Hastings spoke slowly, looking out of the window while he repeated what Tonya had told her mother about the white men and their pickup, and the rope and the trees, and being hurt when they got on her. Hastings stopped when he heard the sound of the approaching ambulance.

Carl Lee walked out of the house with his daughter in his arms. He whispered gently to her, the tears rolling down his face. He walked to the back of the ambulance and stepped inside. The doctor closed the door and carefully took her from him.

♦

Ozzie Walls was the only black sheriff in Mississippi. He was proud of this, especially since Ford County was 74 percent white and the other black sheriffs had been from much blacker counties. He arrested Billy Ray Cobb and Willard in Huey's, a bar on Highway 365 near the lake outside town. They had been there all evening, drinking whiskey and telling everybody about the good time they had been having. Bad news travels fast, and the story had soon reached the sheriff.

Ozzie was smiling when he walked to the table where Cobb was sitting with Willard and two others.

"I'm sorry, sir, but we don't allow niggers in here," said Cobb, and the four started to laugh. Ozzie continued to smile.

When the laughing stopped, Ozzie said, "You boys having a good time, Billy Ray?"

"We were."

"Looks like it. I hate to interrupt your conversation, but you and Mr. Willard need to come with me."

"Where're we going?" Willard asked.

"For a ride."

"I ain't moving," said Cobb. Willard stared desperately at Cobb. Cobb drank his beer and said, "I ain't going to jail."

Ozzie's deputy passed the sheriff the longest, blackest police stick ever used in Ford County. Ozzie struck the center of the table, sending beer and cans in all directions. Willard sat up as if he had been hit. He put his wrists together and held them out for Deputy Looney. He was dragged outside and thrown into a police car.

Cobb did not move. Ozzie took him by the hair and lifted him from his chair, then pushed his face into the floor. He put a knee into his back, slid his stick under his throat, and pulled upward while pushing down on the knee. Cobb stopped moving when he couldn't breathe any more.

He was no trouble after that. Ozzie dragged Cobb by the hair across the dance floor, out of the door, across the yard and threw him into the back seat with Willard.

♦

Jake Brigance woke at 5.30 a.m. as usual, rolled out of bed, and went downstairs to make coffee for his wife, Carla. She was still asleep. He had to be at the Coffee Shop at 6 a.m. He had made many rules like this for himself. He was ambitious but poor. If he was going to be the most successful lawyer in the state, he knew he would also have to be the hardest working.

He gave Carla her coffee, kissed his still sleeping four-year-old daughter goodbye, and went out of the house. The new red Saab he drove had a lot in common with the beautiful nineteenth-century house he had just left. First, they were the only ones of their kind in Ford County. Second, he owed the three local banks a lot of money for both of them. There were good reasons why Jake Brigance worked so hard.

He heard about the rape of Tonya Hailey at the Coffee Shop, as he was eating breakfast with Tim Nunley, who worked at the local garage, and Bill and Bert West, who worked at the shoe factory north of town. There were three deputies having breakfast at the next table, and they asked him if he had defended Billy Ray Cobb on a drugs case a few years ago.

"No, I didn't represent him. I think he had a Memphis lawyer," Jake replied. "What's he done?"

"We arrested him last night for rape."

"Rape!"

"Yes, him and Pete Willard."

"Who did they rape?"

"You remember that Hailey nigger you looked after in that murder trial a few years ago?"

"Lester Hailey? Of course I remember."

"You know his brother Carl Lee?"

"Sure. Know him well. I know all the Haileys. Represented most of them."

"Well, it was his little girl."

"You're joking?"

"No."

Suddenly Jake didn't feel hungry any more. He pushed his plate to one side. He listened to the conversation change from fishing to Japanese cars and back to fishing.

♦

At three minutes before seven, Jake unlocked the front door to his office and turned on the lights. His office was a two-story building in a row of two-story buildings overlooking the courthouse on the north side of the square, just down from the Coffee Shop. The building had been built by the Wilbanks family back in the 1890s, when they owned most of Ford County. There had been a Wilbanks practicing law in the building until 1979, when Jake's employer, Lucien Wilbanks, had been thrown out of the legal profession for a series of offenses resulting from a serious drink problem.

Lucien had been more hurt by this than anything that had happened to him in his troubled life. He gave the keys of the office to Jake and left town. The firm was now Jake's and though Lucien had come back, he had no involvement with it. He spent most of his time up at the Wilbanks' place, drinking whiskey and looking out over the garden.

♦

Carl Lee had not been able to sleep at the hospital. Tonya's condition was serious but she was not going to die. They had seen her at midnight, after the doctor warned them that she looked bad. She did. Gwen had kissed the little bandaged face while Carl Lee stood at the end of the bed, unable to do anything but stare at the small figure surrounded by machines, tubes, and nurses.

The sheriff, Ozzie Clark, brought coffee and cakes at two in the morning, and told Carl Lee all he knew about Cobb and Willard.

♦

Jake began to check his mail. He heard his secretary Ethel Twitty come in at eight-thirty as usual. At around that time Sheriff Ozzie Clarke was typing up Pete Willard's story of the rape.

Ozzie had told Willard what had happened to the last white man who had gone to the State Jail at Parchman.

"About five years ago a young white man in Helena County raped a black girl. She was twelve. They were waiting for him when he got to Parchman. Knew he was coming. On his first night about thirty blacks tied him over a big oil drum and climbed on. The guards watched and laughed. They hate rapists. The other prisoners got him every night for three months, and then they killed him."

After that, Willard seemed to want to help the sheriff as much as he could.

Chapter 2   Revenge

Jake was in court the next day to see Billy Ray and Willard go before the local judge and to hear Ozzie Clarke's report of Willard's story. Carl Lee was there too. As soon as they had heard the judge say that the two men should be kept in jail, Carl Lee and Jake walked out of the courtroom and down to the first floor. They stopped at the back door of the court.

6

They talked about Tonya and Carl Lee's family. Then Carl Lee told Jake that his younger brother Lester was coming down from Chicago.

"What's Lester coming in for?" Jake asked.

"Family business."

"Are you two planning something?"

"No. He just wants to see Tonya."

"You two be careful."

"That's easy for you to say, Jake."

"I know."

"You've got a little girl. If she was lying up in the hospital, beaten and raped, what would you do?"

Jake looked through the window of the door and could not answer. Carl Lee waited.

"Don't do anything stupid, Carl Lee."

"Answer my question. What would you do?"

"I don't know. I don't know what I'd do."

"Let me ask you this. If it was your little girl, and if it was two niggers, and you could get your hands on them, what would you do?"

"Kill them."

Carl Lee smiled, then laughed.

"I'm sure you would, Jake. I'm sure you would. Then you'd hire an expensive lawyer to say you were crazy, just like you did when you defended Lester."

As they came out of the courthouse, Jake told Carl Lee it had been different when Lester was on trial. There was no planning. The man Lester had killed had attacked him first. Carl Lee looked back up at the stairs.

"Is this how they'll come into the courtroom?" he asked, without looking at Jake.

"Who?"

7

"Those boys."

"Yes. Most of the time they take them up those stairs. It's quicker and safer. They can park right outside the door here."

"Are you ready to defend another member of my family?"

"Don't do it, Carl Lee. It's not worth it. What if you're found guilty and they give you the electric chair? What about your children? Who'll look after them?"

"I have no choice, Jake. I'll never sleep till those two are dead. I owe it to my little girl, I owe it to myself, and I owe it to my people. It'll be done."

They opened the doors, and walked down to Washington Street, opposite Jake's office. They shook hands. Jake promised to stop at the hospital the next day to see Gwen and the family.

"One more thing, Jake. Will you meet me at the jail when they arrest me?"

Jake nodded before he thought about what Carl Lee was saying. Carl Lee smiled and walked down the sidewalk to his pickup.

♦

Carl Lee's younger brother, Lester, drove from Chicago to Clanton in his new Cadillac. It was late Wednesday night when he arrived at the hospital. He found some of his cousins reading magazines in the second-floor waiting room. When he saw Carl Lee, he pulled him close and held him tightly. They had not seen each other since the Christmas holidays, when half the blacks in Chicago traveled home to Mississippi and Alabama.

"How is she?" Lester asked.

"Better. Much better. Might go home this weekend."

Lester felt his breathing get easier. When he had left Chicago eleven hours earlier he had thought she was near death. He lit a cigarette under the NO SMOKING sign and stared at his big brother. "You OK?"

Carl Lee nodded. He looked down the hall.

"Come outside," he said. "I've got some things to ask you."

◆

The Ford County Courthouse opened at 8 a.m. and closed at 5 p.m. every day except Friday, when it closed at four-thirty. At four-thirty on Friday, Carl Lee was hiding in a first-floor toilet. He sat and listened quietly for an hour. No one. Silence. He walked through the wide, dark hall to the back doors, and looked through the window. There was no one around. He listened for a while. No one.

He started to study the building. He pretended to be on trial. He put his hands behind him and walked the thirty feet to the stairs – up the stairs, ten steps, then a turn to the left, just like Lester said. He had a good memory, and Lester's time in the army had made him good at giving directions.

Carl Lee studied the courthouse for over an hour. Up and down, up and down, he followed the movements that would be made by the men who had raped his daughter. He followed them in his mind, room by room. He sat in the judge's chair and looked out over the court. He sat in one of the comfortable chairs in the jury box. He sat in the witness chair.

It was dark at seven o'clock when Carl Lee Hailey raised a window in the toilet and went quietly through the bushes and into the darkness.

◆

Getting the gun was no problem. Carl Lee and Lester just went to Memphis, met an old army friend of Carl Lee's called Cat Bruster and asked for an M-16.* Two hours later it was in the

* M-16: an automatic weapon used by the US army.

trunk of Lester's Cadillac. The gun was the easy part; what came next would be harder.

◆

On May 20, Billy Ray Cobb and Pete Willard were brought back to the court to hear Judge Bullard tell them the date of their trial. Jake Brigance had no reason to be in court, but he still worried about Carl Lee as he worked in his office.

Just before two o'clock he went over to the window one more time and lit another cigarette. The two rapists had just heard that they would be held in the county jail until the trial.

The crowd started to leave the courtroom, but Carl Lee's brother, Lester, did not move. He watched closely as the two white boys were taken through the door into the room behind the judge's table. When they were out of sight, he placed his head in his hands and said a short prayer. Then he listened.

◆

Cobb went first down the stairs, then Willard, then Deputy Looney. Ten steps down, then turn right. Then ten steps to the first floor. Three other deputies waited outside by the police cars, smoking and watching the reporters who had come to the court.

When Cobb reached the second step from the floor, with Willard three steps behind, and Looney one step behind him, a small door burst open and Carl Lee Hailey jumped out from the darkness with the M-16 in his hands.

Holding the gun only one or two feet from the men who had raped his daughter, he opened fire. The loud, rapid gunfire shook the courthouse and broke the silence. The rapists froze, then screamed as they were hit – Cobb first, in the stomach and chest, then Willard, in the face, neck, and throat. They tried to run back up the stairs, but fell over each other as they slipped on their own blood.

Deputy Looney was hit in the leg but managed to get up the stairs into a back room. From there he could hear the screams of Cobb and Willard, and the crazy nigger laughing. Bullets continued to hit the walls of the narrow stairway, and as he looked through the door, Looney could see blood and flesh sliding down the walls.

The enormous explosions of the M-16 filled the courthouse. Through the gunfire and the sounds of the bullets hitting the walls of the stairway, Looney could still hear Carl Lee's crazy laughter.

When Carl Lee stopped, he threw the gun at the two bodies and ran into the toilet. He went out through the window, as he had done on that earlier evening, onto the sidewalk. Then he walked to his pickup and drove home.

Cobb, or what was left of him, stopped moving and lay against Willard. Their blood mixed and ran down each step, covering the foot of the stairway.

◆

Jake ran across the street to the back door of the courthouse. One deputy was on the floor, a gun in his hand, shouting at the reporters who were trying to get in. The other deputies looked out from behind the police cars. Jake ran to the front of the courthouse, where more deputies were guarding the door and getting people out of the building.

Jake pushed his way through the crowd and inside. There he found Ozzie Clarke directing people and shouting instructions to his men. He called to Jake, and they walked down the hall to the back of the court, where a half dozen deputies stood, guns in hand, looking silently at the stairway. Jake felt sick. The front of

Willard's head was missing. Cobb had taken most of the bullets in his back. The thick smell of gunfire hung over the stairway.

"Jake, you'd better leave," Ozzie said, without taking his eyes off the bodies.

"Why?"

"Just leave."

"Why?"

"Because we've got to take pictures and stuff, and you don't need to be here."

"OK. But you don't question him without me there. Understand?"

Ozzie nodded.

◆

The only vehicles outside the Hailey house were Gwen's car, Carl Lee's pickup, and the red Cadillac from Illinois. Ozzie expected no trouble as the police cars parked in a row across the front yard. The deputies bent down behind the open doors, watching as the sheriff walked alone to the house. He stopped. The front door opened slowly and the Hailey family came out.

The two groups watched each other, each waiting for the other to say or do something, each wanting to avoid what had to happen. Ozzie kicked at some dirt on the path, looking at the family, then at his men.

Finally, he said, "You'd better come with me."

Carl Lee looked at the sheriff but did not move. Gwen and the boy cried as Lester took the girl from her daddy. Then Carl Lee knelt in front of the three boys and whispered to them again that he must leave but he wouldn't be gone long. He held them close, and they all cried and held on to him. He turned and kissed his wife, then walked down the steps to the sheriff.

Chapter 3   Afterward

"You can see him in a minute, Jake," Ozzie said, after Carl Lee had been brought back to the sheriff's office.

"Thanks. You sure he did it?"

"Yes, I'm sure."

"He didn't say he did it?"

"No. He didn't say anything. I guess Lester told him what to do."

Half an hour later, lawyer and client sat across the table and looked at each other carefully. They smiled but neither spoke. They had last talked five days before – the day after the rape.

Carl Lee was not as troubled now. His face was relaxed and his eyes were clear. Finally he said:

"You didn't think I'd do it, Jake."

"Not really. You did do it?"

"You know I did."

Jake smiled, nodded, and crossed his arms.

"How do you feel?"

Carl Lee sat back in the folding chair.

"Well, I feel better. I don't feel good about the whole thing. But then I don't feel good about what happened to my girl, you know?"

"Are you scared?"

"Of what?"

"How about the electric chair?"

"No, Jake, that's why I've got you. I don't plan to go to the chair. You helped Lester, now you can do it for me, Jake."

"It's not quite that easy, Carl Lee. You just don't shoot a person, or two people, tell the jury they needed to be killed, and expect to walk out of the courtroom."

"You did with Lester."

"But every case is different. And the big difference here is that you killed two white boys and Lester killed a nigger. Big difference."

"You scared, Jake?"

"Why should I be scared? I'm not facing the electric chair."

"You don't sound too confident."

You big, stupid fool, thought Jake. How could he be confident at a time like this? Sure, he was confident before the killings, but now it was different. His client was facing the electric chair for a crime which everyone knew he did. And that was only the beginning of his problems. Carl Lee was a black who had killed two whites in a mainly white county, Rufus Buckley would be the prosecutor, and Rufus would do everything he could to win. It was personal between him and Jake. And there was going to be a problem about money.

Jake hated to discuss professional costs, but he knew he had to do it immediately. Clients wanted to know about his charges, and most were shocked at how expensive the law could be. After he had talked about Carl Lee's family and how they were, Jake started to talk about preparing for the trial. Carl Lee made it easy for him and asked how much all of that was going to cost.

Jake looked at the file and the contract he had brought with him and thought desperately of a fair amount. There were other lawyers out there who would take such a case for almost nothing – nothing except publicity. He thought about the land Carl Lee owned, the job at the paper factory, and his family, and finally said, "Ten thousand."

Carl Lee did not seem too worried, though he said, "You charged Lester five thousand."

They finally agreed on seven thousand, five hundred. After Jake filled out the contract and Carl Lee signed, Carl Lee asked:

"Jake, how much would you charge a man with plenty of money?"

"Fifty thousand."

"Fifty thousand! Are you serious?"

"Yes."

"Man, that's a lot of money. Did you ever get that much?"

"No, but I haven't seen too many people on trial for murder with that kind of money."

Once he had finished talking with his client, Jake left the sheriff's office and walked toward the reporters with their microphones and cameras. Although he pretended he wanted to get away from them, he stopped for enough time to stand in front of the cameras and answer ten or more questions. Ozzie and the deputies watched from inside.

"Jake loves cameras," the sheriff said.

"All lawyers do," added one of the deputies.

♦

After a cold supper, Jake and his wife sat at the front of their house and looked out at the garden. They talked about the case. Jake's interview was too late for the early evening news, so he and Carla waited for the ten o'clock program. And there he was, looking fit and handsome. Jake thought he looked great on TV and he was excited to be there. He felt good. He enjoyed the publicity. And when Carl Lee Hailey was found not guilty of the murder of the two white men who raped his daughter, before an all-white jury in rural Mississippi . . .

"What're you smiling about?" asked Carla.

"Nothing."

"Sure. You're thinking about the trial, and the cameras, and the reporters, and walking out of the courthouse with Carl Lee a free man, reporters chasing you with the TV cameras, everyone congratulating you. I know exactly what you're thinking about."

"Then why did you ask?"

"To see if you'd admit it."

"OK. I admit it. This case could make me famous and make us a million dollars."

"If you win."

◆

Next morning, Tuesday, Jake ate his usual breakfast at the Coffee Shop. He noticed that some of the regular customers were quieter with him than normal, but he hoped this would change when Deputy Looney was out of hospital. Looney was well liked by the other customers, and Jake knew that there were some who would not be happy about him defending Carl Lee. He spent the rest of the morning making arrangements for the trial, and talking to a TV reporter from Memphis. He went home feeling a lot happier.

◆

On Wednesday, at 10 a.m., the two rapists were buried. The minister struggled desperately for something comforting to say to the small crowd. The service was short and with few tears.

Afterward, friends came to the Cobb's house. The men sat around in the back yard while the women looked after Mrs. Cobb. The men drank whiskey and talked about the good times when niggers knew their place. Then one cousin said he knew someone who used to be active in the Ku Klux Klan,* and he might give him a call. Cobb's grandfather had been in the Klan, the cousin explained, and when he and Billy Ray were children the old man told stories about hanging niggers in Ford and Tyler

* Ku Klux Klan: a secret organization that began in 1865 in the southern states of the United States and has a long history of violent attacks against black people and their supporters. Its members wear white robes, tall hats, and masks.

Counties. They should do the same thing the nigger had done. Maybe the Klan would be interested.

◆

In the courtroom, the groups of blacks and whites sat opposite each other and watched the machinery of justice at work. Ozzie Walls was the first witness. He gave a clear report of what had happened when Cobb and Willard were killed and what had happened after. He talked about the shooting, the bodies, the wounds, the gun, the fingerprints on the gun and the fingerprints of the defendant. Other witnesses followed and told how they had seen Carl Lee shoot the two men and walk out of the courthouse.

It was clear that he had killed the men who raped his daughter, and Jake did not ask any questions. Carl Lee was handed to the sheriff to be held until the trial, and everyone left the courtroom. Jake got ready to talk to the reporters who had already started to crowd around the courtroom doors.

Later on Wednesday night, the doctors had to remove Looney's leg below the knee. They called Ozzie at the jail, and he told Carl Lee.

◆

Rufus Buckley looked through the Thursday morning papers and read with great interest the report of the previous day's events in Ford County. He was delighted to see his name mentioned by the reporters and by Mr. Brigance. He didn't like Brigance, but he was glad Jake used his name in front of the cameras and reporters. For two days Brigance and Carl Lee had had all the publicity: it was time the prosecutor was mentioned.

Rufus Buckley was forty-one, and very ambitious. He wanted a big public position – maybe, even, Governor. He had it all planned, but he was not well known outside the district. He needed to be seen, and heard. He needed publicity. Rufus needed, more than anything else, to win a big, nasty, well-publicized murder trial.

◆

On the same Thursday morning, Jake was reading the same newspaper. He was interrupted by his secretary, Ethel, who came and stood in front of the big desk.

"Mr. Brigance, my husband and I received a threatening phone call last night, and I've just had the second one here at the office. I don't like this."

Jake pointed to a chair.

"Sit down, Ethel. What did these people say?"

"They threatened me because I work for you. Said I'd be sorry because I worked for a nigger lover. They threatened to harm you and your family too. I'm just scared."

Jake was worried too, but did not show it to Ethel. He had called Ozzie on Wednesday and reported the calls to his own house.

He advised her to change her number, but she did not want to do that. She wanted him to stop defending Carl Lee. Jake refused, and the conversation ended, like so many conversations he had with Ethel, in disagreement.

An hour later, Ethel called him to say that Lucien, the man who had given Jake the law business, had asked Jake to come to his house with some recent cases. Lucien came to the office or called once a month. He read cases and kept up to date with developments in the law. He had little else to do except drink his whiskey. He looked forward to Jake's monthly visits, when he could hear about the world he used to work in and give advice to the only man who now listened to him. The advice was, in fact, surprisingly good, and Jake could never understand how Lucien knew so much.

Later on Thursday, therefore, Jake parked the Saab behind Lucien's old Porsche, walked up to the house and handed the cases to him. Lucien offered whiskey, then wine, then beer, but Jake did not accept any. Carla did not like drinking, and Lucien knew it.

"Congratulations."

"For what?" Jake asked.

"For the Hailey case."

"Why are you congratulating me?"

"I never had such a big case, and I had some big ones."

"What do you mean by 'big'?"

"Lots of publicity. That's what makes a lawyer successful, Jake. If you're unknown, you don't eat. When people get in trouble, they call a lawyer – and they call someone they've heard of. You must sell yourself to the public. And you've got to try to get the trial moved to another county. Without enough blacks on the jury, you won't have a chance! This county is 26 percent black. Every other county in the district is at least 30 percent black. Van Buren County is 40 percent, that means more black jurors. If the trial is here, there's a risk of an all-white jury, and believe me, I've seen enough all-white juries in this county. At the very least you need one black."

Jake felt that it was not going to be easy to get Judge Noose to move the trial, and said so to Lucien.

"That's not a problem," he replied. "The main thing is to ask. Then, when they find that poor man guilty, you can claim he did not have a fair trial because the judge refused to move."

"So you don't feel too optimistic about Carl Lee's chances."

Lucien thought for a moment.

"Not really. It will be difficult."

"Why?"

"Looks like it was planned. Right?"

"Yes."

"I'm sure you'll say he was insane."

"I don't know."

"You must," said Lucien. "There is no other possible defense. You can't say it was an accident. You can't say he shot those two boys with a machine gun in self-defense, can you?"

"No."

"You won't tell the jury he was at home with his family?"

"Of course not."

"Then what other defense do you have? You *must* say he was crazy!"

"But, Lucien, he was *not* insane, and there's no way I can find a psychiatrist who will say he was. He planned it – every detail."

Lucien smiled and took a drink.

"That's why you're in trouble, my boy – but you're still lucky to have the case."

"You really think so?" asked Jake.

"I'm serious. It's a lawyer's dream. Win it and you're famous. It could make you rich."

"I'll need your help."

"You've got it. I need something to do."

◆

The next day, Friday, Lester came into Jake's office and told him the family could only raise nine hundred dollars to pay for Carl Lee's defense. All of the banks in town had refused to lend money.

"Wonderful," thought Jake. "My family and my secretary are getting threatening phone calls. My best friend tells me I can't win the case, and now I'm only going to get nine hundred dollars for a case which is going to stop me doing any other work for weeks. Wonderful."

Chapter 4   The Klan

Before Carl Lee Hailey could go on trial, he had to go in front of a jury of citizens of Ford County. It was their job to decide if the two murders had happened and if it was reasonable for Carl Lee to stand trial. This was the first opportunity for Rufus Buckley to get some of the publicity he wanted so much.

The grand jury made its decision. There was a case against Carl Lee and he would have to stand trial for murder. It was then Rufus Buckley's turn to stand on the front steps of the courthouse in the middle of a crowd of reporters and cameramen.

Buckley had copies of the legal documents with Carl Lee's name on. He waved these in front of the cameras. He talked like a priest in church, saying how terrible it was for people to take the law into their own hands. He praised the jury for the decision they had made. He accused Carl Lee Hailey of being a lawless man and said he wanted the trial to happen soon. He guaranteed he would prove that Carl Lee Hailey was guilty of murder. He guaranteed Carl Lee Hailey would die on the electric chair. He was rude, unpleasant, self-important. He was himself.

A few of the reporters left, but he did not stop talking. He told those who remained about his skill as a lawyer and his success as a prosecutor. More reporters left. More cameras were turned off. He praised Judge Noose for his wisdom and fairness. He praised the intelligence and good judgment of Ford County jurors.

When he finished speaking, there were no reporters left. They had grown tired of him.

◆

Stump Sisson was the Ku Klux Klan's leader in Mississippi. He had called the meeting at a small hut deep in the forest in Nettles County, two hundred and thirty miles south of Ford County.

There were no special clothes or speeches. The small group of Klansmen discussed the events in Ford County with Freddie Cobb, brother of Billy Ray. Freddie had called a friend, who had contacted Stump to arrange the meeting.

"When's the nigger's trial?"

"I'm not sure," Cobb said. "I think it'll probably be later in summer."

He was most worried, he said, by all the talk about the nigger saying he was insane and going free. It wasn't right. The nigger killed his brother in cold blood, planned the shooting. What could the Klan do about it? Cobb complained that the niggers had so much protection these days that no one could do anything against them.

"Hell, white people ain't got a chance, except for the Klan. Who else will march and stand up for white people? All the laws work to help the niggers. That's why we called the Klan."

"What about your brother. Did he rape her?"

"We're not sure, probably not. Willard, the other one, said he did it, but Billy Ray never did. He always had plenty of women. Why would he rape a little nigger girl? And if he did, what's the big problem?"

"Who's the nigger's lawyer?"

"Brigance, a local boy in Clanton. Young, but pretty good. He told some reporters the nigger would say he was insane and would go free."

"Who's the judge?"

"I don't know yet."

Sisson and the Klan members listened carefully to this mindless farmer. They liked his complaints about the government, but they had also read the papers and watched TV and they knew his brother had received justice. But at the hands of a nigger. It was unthinkable.

The case could be useful to them. With the trial several

months away, there was time to plan. They could march during the day around the courthouse in their Klan uniform of tall hats and masks. The press would love it – hate them, but love the arguments, the anger. And at night they could frighten people with their burning crosses* and threatening phone calls. There would also be violence. They knew what the sight of the Klan did to crowds of angry niggers.

Ford County could be their playground for search and destroy, hit and run. They had time to organize and call in people from other states. The Hailey case could be used to bring together all the Southern whites who still refused to accept the rights of blacks to a place in society.

"Mr. Cobb, can you get us the names and addresses of the nigger, his family, his lawyer, the judge, and the jurors?" asked Sisson.

Cobb thought about this.

"Everybody except the jurors. They ain't been chosen yet. What're you thinking?"

"We're not sure, but the Klan will most likely get involved. We need to remind people we're still here, and this could be a good opportunity."

"Can I help?" Cobb asked.

"Sure, but you'd need to be a member."

"We ain't got any Klan up in Clanton. It stopped meeting a long time ago. My grandfather used to be a member."

"You mean the grandfather of this man was a Klansman?"

"Yes," Cobb answered proudly.

"Well, then we must get involved."

◆

* burning crosses: left by the Ku Klux Klan in front of the houses of people they want to frighten.

Buckley's four o'clock press conference did not come on the early evening news. Jake laughed when first the national TV channels and then Memphis, then Jackson, then Ripelo, ended their broadcasts with no news about the Hailey trial, and no pictures of Buckley on the screen.

At ten, Jake and his wife Carla lay in the dark on the sofa, waiting for the news. Finally, there was Buckley, on the front steps, waving papers and shouting while the reporter explained that this was Rufus Buckley, the man who would prosecute Carl Lee Hailey. The camera was pointed at Buckley for a few seconds, and then the camera moved around the town square to give a wonderful view of the center of Clanton. It finally came back to the reporter for two sentences about a trial in late summer.

"Buckley's really horrible," Carla said, and turned off the sound of the TV. "You know what I dislike most about your murder trials?"

She kicked the cushions off the sofa with her thin, brown, almost perfect legs.

"The blood, the pain?"

"No." She let her shoulder-length hair fall around her as she fell back on the sofa.

"The loss of life?"

"No."

She was wearing one of his old shirts. She began to play with the buttons.

"The horrible possibility of an innocent man facing the electric chair?"

"No."

She unbuttoned the shirt. The blue television screen was the only light in the room. It was enough for Jake to see her almost perfect arms reach out for him.

"The emotion, the desire . . ."

"That's more like it," she said, and slid an almost perfect brown leg up, up, up to the back of the sofa, where it gently came to rest.

They moved closer to each other and she turned off the TV. The room was warm and dark.

Chapter 5   Lawyers

Harry Rex Vonner was enormously fat. He was a lawyer who specialized in cases where marriages had broken down nastily. He could be just as nasty as his cases, and his services were in great demand. He could get you the children, the house, the farm, the dog, everything. One wealthy farmer sent him a check each month so that the woman he was married to (his fourth wife) couldn't hire him for herself. Harry Rex sent his criminal cases to Jake, and Jake sent his nasty marriage problem cases to Harry Rex. They were friends and they disliked other lawyers, especially Rufus Buckley.

On Tuesday morning, Harry Rex came slowly up the stairs to Jake's office. The stairway shook as he climbed to the first floor. He was breathing heavily as he entered the big room.

"Morning, Harry Rex."

"Why don't you get a downstairs office?" he demanded between breaths.

"You need the exercise. If it weren't for those stairs, your weight would be over three hundred pounds."

"Thanks. I just came from the courtroom. Noose wants you there at ten-thirty if possible. Wants to talk about Hailey with you and Buckley. Agree the trial date. He asked me to tell you."

"Good. I'll be there."

"You'll find Buckley there too. You should see him. He's telling everyone about his big TV appearance last night. But no one wants to talk about it. He's like a child begging for attention."

"Be nice to him. He may be your next governor."

"Not if he loses the Hailey case. And he's going to lose Hailey, Jake. We'll pick a good jury, twelve good and faithful citizens. Then we'll buy them."

"I didn't hear that."

"It works every time."

♦

A few minutes after ten-thirty, Jake entered the judge's office behind the courtroom and coolly shook hands with Buckley and the other lawyers. They had been waiting for him. Noose waved him toward a seat and sat behind the desk.

"Jake, this will take just a few minutes. I would like to see Carl Lee Hailey in the morning at nine. Any problems with that?"

"No. That'll be fine," replied Jake.

"OK. Now let's discuss a trial date for Mr. Hailey. As you know, the next term for the court here is in late August, and I'm sure we'll be just as busy then. Because of the nature of this case and, honestly, because of the publicity, I think it would be best if we had a trial as soon as is practical."

"The sooner the better," said Buckley.

"Jake, how long will you need to prepare for trial?"

"Sixty days."

"Sixty days!" Buckley repeated. "Why so long?"

Jake ignored him. He explained to the judge that they would be using an insanity defense and would need Carl Lee to be examined by a psychiatrist, and that all this would take time. Buckley kept shouting that it was unnecessary.

"Relax, Rufus," Jake said calmly. "The cameras will be here in sixty days, even ninety days. They won't forget about you. You can give interviews. Hold press conferences, everything. Don't worry so much. You'll get your chance."

Buckley's face went red. He took three steps in Jake's direction.

"Gentlemen, please," Noose interrupted. "This is going to be a long, emotional case. I expect you to act like professionals. Now, my diary is very full. The only time I have is the week of July 22. Is that a problem?"

Jake smiled at Buckley and looked at his own diary.

"Looks good to me."

◆

After lunch, Jake visited his famous client in Ozzie's office at the jail. He told him the trial was going to start on July 22."

"That's two months away! Why so long?"

"We need the time. It'll take that long to find a psychiatrist who'll say you were crazy. Then Buckley will send you to Whitfield to be seen by the state's psychiatrists, and they'll all say you weren't crazy. It takes time."

"No way to have it sooner?"

"We don't want it sooner."

"And if I do?"

Jake studied him carefully.

"What's the matter, big man?"

"I've got to get out of here, and fast."

"I thought you said jail wasn't so bad."

"It ain't, but I need to get home. Gwen's got no money, she can't find a job. Lester's in trouble with his wife, and I hate to ask my family for help."

"But they will help, won't they?"

"A little. They've got their own problems. You've got to get me out of here, Jake."

Gwen, he said, had less than a hundred dollars. She had to pay bills and they didn't have much food. She had visited on Sunday and cried for an hour. Her family could not help much – maybe some vegetables from the garden and a few dollars for milk and eggs.

Jake looked through his notes and waited for Carl Lee to ask for some of his money back. Most of his poorer clients did. But the question did not come.

"Anything you want to ask, Carl Lee?"

"Yes. What can I say tomorrow when I see the judge?"

"Carl Lee, for the moment you don't say anything. Remember, you paid me to do the talking."

◆

On the Sunday morning, others were thinking about Carl Lee Hailey and his family. At black churches all over Clanton, the buckets and baskets and plates were passed and re-passed and left at the front doors to collect money for the Hailey family. The people who had come to pray were asked to give generously to support Carl Lee and his family. The Reverend Ollie Agee had organized the collection in his church and other churches across town. He was very pleased that the black people of Clanton were giving so much. Another two Sundays like this and the churches would be able to start a strong movement against the nigger haters of Ford County. There might even be enough money to pay for a new Cadillac for some valuable church workers – like the Reverend Ollie Agee.

Carl Lee Hailey gave the blacks really good reasons to work together.

◆

Jake soon discovered that Carl Lee was not the only one with problems. The Ku Klux Klan had decided that it was time to show him their feelings about nigger-loving lawyers. Several hours before the sun rose on Monday morning, three Klan members put up a wooden cross in the front yard of Jake's house on Adams Street and set fire to it. It was a warning.

"This scares you, doesn't it?" Jake asked his wife, as they stared out in horror at the burning cross.

"If they can do this, Jake," Carla replied slowly, "why not the house? No case is worth this. You've got to stop."

Chapter 6   Professional Witnesses

Jake had no intention of dropping the case. First, he had to find a psychiatrist they could afford. He needed to talk to Lucien.

Two days after Jake phoned him, Lucien called Ethel. He asked her to tell Jake to come see him. It was important. He had a visitor that Jake needed to meet.

Dr. W.T. Bass was a retired psychiatrist from Jackson. His retirement had been for the same reasons that Lucien was forbidden to practice law. He had a liking for whiskey that was stronger than his liking for his profession.

The doctor and Lucien sat outside the house, waiting for Jake to arrive.

"What do you want me to do?" asked Dr. Bass.

"Just say he was insane."

"Was he?" asked the doctor.

"That's not important."

"What is important?"

"To give the jury a reason to say Carl Lee was not guilty! They won't care if he's crazy or not. But they'll need some reason to let him go."

"It would be nice to examine him."

"You can. He's at the jail just waiting for someone to talk to."

"I'll need to meet with him several times."

"I know that."

"And if I don't think he was insane at the time of the shooting?"

"Then you won't be able to speak at the trial, and get your name and picture in the paper, and you won't be interviewed on TV."

Bass finished one glass and poured another. He was not happy about taking the case. He didn't practice now and he was frightened of making a fool of himself. He knew his weaknesses.

"What about this?" He waved his drink at Lucien.

"You shouldn't drink so much," Lucien replied, keeping the smile off his face with difficulty.

The doctor dropped his drink and exploded in laughter. He rolled out of his chair holding his stomach, helpless with laughter.

"And now you're drunk," Lucien said, as he went into the house for another bottle.

♦

When Jake arrived an hour later, Lucien and the doctor were asleep. Jake walked up the steps to the house and woke Lucien.

"Jake, my boy, how are you?"

"Fine, Lucien. I see you're doing quite well." He looked at the empty bottle, and one not quite empty.

"I wanted you to meet a man," Lucien said, trying to sit up straight.

"Who is he?"

"Our psychiatrist. Dr. Bass, from Jackson. A good friend. He'll help us with Hailey."

"Is he a good psychiatrist?"

"The best. We've worked together on several insanity cases. He drinks like a fish, but never during a trial."

"That's comforting."

"He wants to meet Hailey as soon as possible. Tomorrow if he can."

The one problem today was that no one could wake Dr. Bass to arrange the meeting. Jake walked down the steps toward his car, listening to his former boss laugh and curse and throw pieces of ice at Dr. W.T. Bass, psychiatrist, witness for the defense.

♦

Deputy DeWayne Looney left the hospital that afternoon, and drove his wife and three children to the jail, where the sheriff, the other deputies, and a few friends waited with a cake and small gifts. He would continue to work in the office, and would keep his uniform and full salary.

Two days later, Carl Lee Hailey was taken to meet Dr. Wilbert Rodeheaver, the head psychiatrist at the state hospital. Dr. Rodeheaver had been appointed by the prosecutor to see if Carl Lee had been insane or not when he killed the men who raped his daughter and accidentally shot Deputy Looney.

Chapter 7   Problems for Jake

Several legal steps were still needed before Carl Lee's trial. First Jake had to ask for the trial to be moved to another part of the state. Although he did not win this argument, he felt OK. He did a good job in court, and looked a lot better than Rufus Buckley, the prosecutor. The problem was, that the judge then decided that there was too much publicity about the case, and told both lawyers they had to stop talking to journalists. He did not want the trial to be held in the newspapers and on TV.

Outside the courthouse it hurt to say no to the reporters. They followed Jake across Washington Street, where he excused himself with a "No comment" and escaped into his office.

The loss of publicity hurt even more when Ethel came in to tell him the firm had big money problems. Since the start of the Hailey case, he had seen no other clients and had not been chasing those who had failed to pay him.

"Look at these," she said, waving a handful of bills under his nose. "Four thousand dollars. How am I supposed to pay these?"

"How much is in the bank?"

"Nineteen hundred dollars. Nothing came in this morning."

"Nothing?"

"Not a penny."

After Ethel had complained for another five minutes about how this case was ruining the business, Jake lost his temper.

"Shut up, Ethel. Just shut up. If you can't take the pressure, then leave. If you can't keep your mouth shut, then you're fired."

"You'd like to fire me, wouldn't you?"

"Maybe I would. I don't care at the moment."

She was a strong, hard woman. Fourteen years with Lucien had done that to her, but at the moment she was clearly very unhappy.

"I'm sorry," she said. "I'm just worried."

"Worried about what?"

"Me and Bud."

"What's wrong with Bud?"

"He's a very sick man."

"I know that."

"His blood pressure is getting worse. Especially after the phone calls. He's scared. We're both scared."

"How many phone calls?"

"Several. They threaten to burn our house or blow it up. They always tell us they know where we live, and if Hailey goes free, then they'll burn it down while we're asleep."

Jake found it difficult to be sympathetic to Ethel – there were other things on his mind. His wife wanted him to drop this case. He knew that the bank would not lend him any more money. The Ku Klux Klan were threatening both him and his secretary. And now he could not talk to the newspapers and get the publicity he needed so badly.

◆

The Ford County Ku Klux Klan had its first meeting at midnight on Thursday, July 11 in a field in a forest somewhere in the northern part of the county. The six new members stood nervously in front of the enormous burning cross and repeated strange words after the leader. An armed guard stood quietly down the road, sometimes looking at the ceremony, but mainly watching for uninvited guests. There were none.

At exactly midnight the six fell to their knees and closed their eyes as white cloths were placed over their heads. They were Klansmen now, these six – and among them was Freddie Cobb, brother of the dead rapist.

◆

A few hours later, Pirtle, the deputy on night duty at the sheriff's office, received a phone call. The caller did not give a name, but he said that the Klan was planning to blow up Jake Brigance's house that night. Pirtle woke the sheriff, and within ten minutes of the call Ozzie Wall and two deputies were outside Jake's house. They checked that there was no one around, then Ozzie pressed the doorbell.

The wooden door opened, and Jake looked out at the sheriff.

He was wearing a nightshirt that fell just below his knees, and he held a loaded gun in his right hand.

"What is it, Ozzie?" he asked.

"Can I come in?"

"Yes. What's going on?"

"Stay outside and wait for me," Ozzie told the deputies.

Ozzie closed the front door behind them and turned off the light. They sat in the dark living-room overlooking the front yard. Ozzie told Jake what the Klan were planning to do – and told him to get his wife and daughter out of town as soon as he could. Jake had never moved so fast in his life. Within fifteen minutes, Carla and their daughter were in the car and driving to a neighbor's house. Ozzie, Jake, and the deputies sat outside in the dark, waiting for the Klan to come.

They didn't have to wait long. Ozzie saw him first, a man walking down the street. In his hand he carried a box – a suitcase of some sort. Ozzie took out his handgun and stick and watched the man walk directly toward him.

Suddenly, the figure ran across the yard next door and to the side of Jake's house. He carefully laid the small suitcase under Jake's bedroom window. As he turned to run, Ozzie's police stick crashed across the side of his head, tearing his right ear into two pieces. He screamed and fell to the ground.

"What's your name?" Ozzie demanded.

The man said nothing.

"I asked you a question," Ozzie said. Pirtle and Nesbit stood beside him, guns ready, too frightened to speak or move.

"I ain't speaking," came the reply.

Ozzie raised the stick high over his head and brought it down on the man's right ankle. They could all hear the bone crack. He screamed and Ozzie kicked him in the face. He fell backward and his head hit the side of the house.

Jake looked at the suitcase and then put his ear next to it.

He jumped back. "It's ticking," he said weakly.

Ozzie bent over the man and laid the police stick softly against his nose.

"I've got one more question before I break every bone in your body. What's in the case?"

No answer.

Ozzie pulled back the stick and broke the man's other ankle.

"What's in the case?" he shouted.

"Dynamite!" came the reply.

Ozzie tied the man to a gas pipe next to the window. He carefully lifted the suitcase by the handle and placed it neatly between the man's broken legs. Ozzie kicked both legs to spread them. Ozzie, the deputies, and Jake backed away slowly and watched him. The man began to cry.

"I don't know how to stop it," he said.

"You'd better learn fast," Jake said.

"Give me some light. And I need both hands," he said.

"Try it with one," Ozzie said.

They waited on the other side of the street, saying little, listening for any unusual noise. After about fifteen minutes, the man shouted and they ran back across the front yard. The empty suitcase had been thrown a few feet away. Next to the man was a neat pile of twelve sticks of dynamite. Between his legs was a large, round-faced clock with wires connected to it.

Ozzie bent down and removed the clock and the wires. He did not touch the dynamite.

"Where are your friends?"

No answer.

He took out his stick again and moved closer to the man.

"I'm going to start breaking bones one at a time. You'd better start talking. Now – where are your friends?"

No answer.

Ozzie stood and quickly looked around. Not at Jake and the deputies, but at the house next door. Seeing nothing, he raised the stick. The man's left arm was still tied to the gas pipe, and Ozzie hit him just above the elbow. The man screamed and pulled to the left. Jake almost felt sorry for him.

"Where are they?" Ozzie demanded.

No answer.

Jake turned his head as the sheriff hit the man again.

"Where are they?"

No answer.

Ozzie raised the stick.

"Stop . . . please stop," the man shouted.

"Where are they?"

"Down that way, about two streets."

"Get the cars," Ozzie ordered.

♦

Two hours later, Jake was in the sheriff's office. His wife and daughter were already on a plane to the town where Carla's parents lived – five hundred miles away. Carla had returned to the house to pack, but had not spoken a word to him. There was no doubt that she blamed him for the danger they had all been in. Jake was happy that his family was alive, but still shook when he thought about what nearly happened. He smiled at Ozzie.

"You play rough, don't you?"

"Only when I have to. I didn't hear you object."

"No, I wanted to help. What about his friend?"

"We found him sleeping in a red pickup about a half a mile from your house."

"Where is he?"

"Hospital. Same room as the other."

"My God, Ozzie. Did you break his legs too?"

"Jake, my friend, he did not cooperate with the police. We had to encourage him."

Chapter 8   The Research Assistant

After talking with Ozzie Walls, Jake went to Lucien's house. He was lonely and unhappy. He had financial problems, his wife and child had gone, he had not slept for twenty-four hours. When Lucien offered him a beer, he drank it quickly and accepted another and then another. By the end of the afternoon, he was drunk. By the end of the evening, he was unconscious.

The next day he woke with the worst headache he had ever had in his life. He was not a man who drank a lot. In fact the last time he had felt like this was when he was a law student. The way he felt now reminded him of the many reasons why he did not like to drink!

♦

Later in the morning, Jake was sitting at his desk, looking out at the courthouse. He still had a bad headache and could not work. Now he had to start to prepare for the most important case of his life with no money in the bank, a drunk law partner, a drunk psychiatrist – and this headache!

He was still sitting there when he heard someone knocking at the door downstairs. He ignored it for fifteen minutes, but whoever it was knew that he was there. He walked to the window and looked out.

"Who is it?" he shouted at the street.

A woman stepped back from the sidewalk under the window

and leaned on a black BMW parked next to the Saab. Her hands were deep in the pockets of old, well-fitting jeans. The midday sun lit up her gold-red hair.

"Are you Jake Brigance?" she asked.

"Yes. What do you want?"

"I need to talk to you."

"I'm very busy."

"It's very important. I just need five minutes of your time."

Jake unlocked the door. She walked in and shook his hand.

"I'm Ellen Roark."

He pointed to a seat by the door.

"Nice to meet you. Sit down." Jake sat on the edge of Ethel's desk. "One sound or two?"

"I beg your pardon?"

She had a quick, northeastern accent, but you could also hear she had spent some time in the South.

"Is it Rork or Row Ark?"

"R-o-a-r-k. That's Rork in Boston, and Row Ark in Mississippi."

"Mind if I call you Ellen?"

"Please do. And can I call you Jake?"

"Yes, please."

"Good, I hadn't planned to call you Mr. Brigance."

"So you come from Boston?"

"Yes, I was born there. Went to Boston College. My dad is Sheldon Roark, a well-known criminal lawyer in Boston."

"I guess I've missed him. What brings you to Mississippi?"

"I'm in law school."

"Well, now that we know each other, what brings you to Clanton?"

"Carl Lee Hailey."

"I'm not surprised."

"I'll finish law school in December, I'm killing time in Oxford this summer, and I'm bored."

Jake smiled and studied her carefully.

"What makes you think I need help?"

"I know you practice alone, and I know you don't have a law clerk."

"What qualifications do you bring with you?"

"I come from a very intelligent family. Last summer I spent three months with the Southern Prisoners' Defense Movement in Birmingham and helped with seven murder trials. In my spare time I write reports for organizations that give free legal advice. I was brought up in my father's law office, and I was a good legal researcher before I could drive. I'm twenty-five years old, and when I grow up I want to be a great criminal lawyer like my dad. Also, my father is very rich and I've got more money than you, so I'll work without charge. A free law clerk for three weeks. I'll do all the research, typing, answering the phone. I'll even carry your papers and make the coffee."

"I was afraid you'd want to be a partner in my firm."

"No. I'm a woman, and I'm in the South. I know my place."

"Why are you so interested in this case?"

"I want to be in the courtroom. I love criminal trials. Big trials where it's a question of life or death. It's a trial lawyer's dream. I just want to be there. I'll stay out of the way, I promise. Just let me work with you and watch the trial."

"Judge Noose hates women lawyers."

"So does every male lawyer in the South. Besides, I'm not a lawyer. I'm a law student."

"I'll let you explain that to him."

"So I've got the job?"

"Yes, you've got the job. I could use some free research. These cases are complicated."

She gave a beautiful, confident smile. "When do I start?"

♦

After he had shown her round the office it was time for lunch, so Jake took Ellen Roark with him to the Coffee Shop. As they ate he looked across at her. Her face was gentle and pleasant with an easy smile. She was not beautiful, but she was intelligent and amazingly attractive. For the first time in two days, Jake began to think he might live. They talked about his plans for the defense. Jake asked her how *she* would do it.

"Well, from what I hear, our client carefully planned the killings and shot them in cold blood, six days after the rape. It sounds exactly like he knew what he was doing. Insanity is our only defense. And it sounds impossible to prove."

"Are you familiar with the insanity defense?" Jake asked.

"Yes. Do we have a psychiatrist?"

"We do and we don't. He'll say anything we want him to say – that is, if he's not drunk at the trial. One of your more difficult jobs will be to make sure that he isn't. It won't be easy, believe me."

"I love new experiences in the courtroom."

"All right, Row Ark. Take a pen. Your boss is now going to give you instructions."

She began making notes on the paper tablecloth.

Chapter 9   Preparations

In early July, Judge Noose instructed Jean, the court clerk, to contact one hundred and fifty voters as possible jury members. The defense had asked for a large number from which to select the twelve, and Noose agreed. Jean and two deputy clerks spent

40

Saturday studying the list of voters, selecting possible people. Noose also told Jean that she must not give the list to anyone – not even her old friend Jake Brigance. This trial was too important to give the Klan a chance to start frightening possible jurors – or to let the lawyers start choosing the jurors before the day of jury selection.

However, Judge Noose did not know about Harry Rex Vonner's ability to get hold of information. At ten o'clock the next day, Harry Rex pushed open the door of Jake's office and threw a copy of the jury list onto his desk.

"Don't ask," he said.

Beside each name he had made notes: "Don't know," "Hates niggers," or "Works at the shoe factory – probably against Carl Lee."

Jake read each name slowly, trying to remember faces or the kind of person they were. There were only names – no addresses, ages, jobs. Most of the names sounded white.

"What do you think?" asked Harry Rex.

"Hard to tell. Mostly white, but we expected that. Where did you get this?"

"I already said – don't ask. I know twenty-six names. That's the best I can do."

"You're a true friend, Harry Rex."

"I'm a prince. Are you ready for the trial?"

"Not yet. But I've found a secret weapon."

"What?"

"You'll meet her later."

◆

As they finished their conversation, Ellen Roark came into the office.

"Good morning, Row Ark," Jake said. "I want you to meet a good friend, Harry Rex Vonner."

Harry Rex shook her hand and looked her up and down – he clearly thought she was very attractive.

"Nice to meet you. What was your first name?"

"Call her Row Ark," Jake said. "She'll clerk here until the Hailey trial's finished."

"That's nice," said Harry Rex – still looking at Ellen, not at Jake.

"Harry Rex is a local lawyer, Row Ark. And one of the many you cannot trust."

"What did you hire a female law clerk for, Jake?" he asked.

"Row Ark's brilliant in criminal law, like most third-year law students. And she's very cheap."

"Do you have something against females, sir?" Ellen asked.

"No ma'am. I love females. I've married four of them."

She looked at his big, dirty shoes, the cheap socks that had dropped around his ankles, his dirty cotton trousers, his old dark blue jacket, his pink wool tie that fell a long way above his fat stomach, and she said to Jake, "I think he's sweet!"

"I might make you wife number five," Harry Rex said.

"The attraction is purely physical," she said.

"Careful," Jake said. "There's been no sex in this office since Lucien left! How's the research?"

"There are dozens of insanity cases, and they're all very long, I've done about half. I planned to work on the others here."

Harry Rex moved toward the door.

"Nice meeting you, Row Ark. I'll see you around."

"Thanks, Harry Rex," said Jake. "See you soon."

◆

Three miles from Jake's office was a small, neat white country house where Ethel and Bud Twitty had lived for almost forty years. It was a pleasant house with pleasant memories of raising children who were now living in the North.

The house was quieter now. Bud hadn't worked for years, not since his first illness in 1975, when he had had a heart attack, followed by two more. He knew that he would not live long, and he had accepted the fact. On Monday night, he sat on the front porch listening to the football game on the radio. Ethel was working in the kitchen. Toward the end of the ball game, he heard a noise. He turned the sound down on the radio. Probably just a dog. Then another noise. He stood and looked toward the garden.

Suddenly, an enormous figure in black with red, white, and black war paint across his face jumped onto the porch and pulled Bud to the ground. Bud's shout for help was not heard in the kitchen. Another man joined the first one and they pulled the old man down the steps and into the garden. One held him and the other hit him in the stomach and face. Within seconds he was unconscious.

Ethel heard noises and ran through the front door. She was caught by a third member of the gang, who twisted her arm violently behind her, and put his hand over her mouth. She couldn't scream or talk or move, and was held there watching the two men beat her husband. On the sidewalk ten feet behind the violence stood three figures, each wearing the white Klan robes. They came out of the darkness and watched the beating.

After an impossibly long, horrible minute the beating slowed down. "Enough," said the white figure in the middle. The men left and Ethel ran down the steps and held her unconscious husband in her arms.

◆

Jake left the hospital after midnight. Bud was still alive, but he had suffered another serious heart attack as well as the broken bones.

Ethel had shouted and screamed at Jake, blaming him for everything.

"You said there was no danger!" she screamed. "It's all your fault!"

Jake had looked around the small waiting room at the friends and relatives. All eyes were on him. Yes, they seemed to say, it was all his fault.

◆

Carl Lee Hailey and his wife were angry too. Gwen had no money to pay her bills, and Carl Lee had no money to pay for his defense, but they had heard that Reverend Agee had collected over six thousand dollars from black churchgoers to help Carl Lee. Why had they not received any of the money yet, they demanded.

Jake had arranged a meeting with Reverend Agee after Gwen visited his office to ask for help with the bills she could no longer pay. He had telephoned the Reverend and asked him to come to his office to talk about the defense. Ozzie Walls had brought Carl Lee across the square too. Reverend Agee had tried to frighten Carl Lee, to tell him he was ungrateful – the church was keeping the money for any future defense. Ozzie helped the Reverend to see that he was making a mistake.

"I agree with Carl Lee and Gwen. Reverend Agee, you ain't done right, and you know it."

"That hurts, Ozzie, coming from you. It really hurts."

"Let me tell you what's going to hurt a lot more than that. Next Sunday, Carl Lee and I will be in your church. Carl Lee will do the talking. He'll tell all your people that the money they've given so generously has not left your pocket – that Gwen and the children are going to lose their house because you're keeping the money people gave. He'll tell them that you lied to them. He may talk for an hour or so. When he's finished, I'll say a few words. I'll tell them what a lying, dishonest nigger you are. I'll tell them about the time you bought that stolen car in Memphis for a hundred dollars and almost got sent to jail. I'll tell them about the money you get from the funeral business. And, Reverend, I'll tell . . ."

"Don't say it, Ozzie," Agee begged.

"I'll tell them a dirty little secret that only you and me and a certain woman of bad character know about."

"When do you want the money?"

"As soon as you can get it," Carl Lee demanded.

Ozzie could be very persuasive sometimes.

♦

The Klan were also making preparations. At around nine o'clock that evening, they met to discuss their next steps. They would have a big march at the beginning of the trial and, like Jake, had been able to get a copy of the list of possible jurors. They planned to visit a few and make sure that they remembered their duty to protect the interests of the white race.

♦

Later that same evening, at Lucien's house, Jake, Ellen, Harry Rex, and Lucien sat round the table on the porch. Lucien, at the head of the table, went through the jury list commenting on every name he recognized. He was drunker than normal.

Chapter 10   The Jury

During the seven days before the trial, the people of Clanton began to feel they were living in a foreign country. First, there were the bus loads of black people who arrived and set up a camp outside the courthouse. Their leader, the Reverend Agee, told the reporters that they would stay until justice was done and Carl Lee was freed. The crowd began to shout: "Free Carl Lee! Free Carl Lee!"

After the blacks came the Klan. They arrived in groups of two and three and came from all over the state. Their leader, Stamp Sisson, was pleased. He drank some whiskey as he checked their dress. He was proud of his men and told them so. This was the biggest meeting of its kind in years, he said. The march could be dangerous, he explained. Niggers could march and scream all day long and no one cared. But if whites tried to march it was dangerous. The niggers could do what they liked, but not white people.

Few people in Clanton had ever seen the Klan march, and as 2 p.m. approached a great wave of excitement went around the square. The shopkeepers and their customers came out to watch, and a group of young blacks gathered under a large tree. Ozzie smelled trouble, but they told him they had only come to watch and listen.

The Klan moved slowly in their white robes and tall pointed masks. Stump walked proudly in front of his men, leading them down the long sidewalk to the center of the square by the courthouse steps.

"You niggers were not invited to this meeting!" Stump screamed into the microphone, pointing at the blacks on the grass. "This is a Klan meeting, not a meeting for niggers!"

As he started to speak, the black people who had gathered around the square started to shout: "Free Carl Lee! Free Carl Lee!"

"Shut up, you wild niggers!" Stump screamed back. "Shut up, you animals!" His men stood facing him, with their backs to the screaming crowd. Ozzie and six deputies moved between the groups.

As the photographers and TV reporters moved in circles, trying to record everything that was happening, no one noticed a small window on the third floor of the courthouse. It opened slowly, and from the darkness a fire-bomb was thrown. It landed perfectly at Stump's feet and exploded. Immediately, the Klan leader's long white robe went up in flames. Stump Sisson was having his five minutes of fame.

The violence which followed the fire-bomb was the worst there had ever been in the small town. Blacks and whites fought with their hands, sticks, and knives, not stopping until Ozzie Walls and his deputies fired their guns in the air. When things became quieter, Ozzie went to the Town Hall. He asked the leader of the town council to contact the Governor. He wanted the National Guard* to be called in. As sheriff he felt the situation was out of control, and he needed the army to help keep order. Clanton had seen nothing like it before.

◆

Jake, Ellen Roark, Harry Rex, and Lucien spent the rest of the week preparing for the trial. They had two main jobs.

The first was to find the people who would make the best jury for Carl Lee. They studied the list of names again and again, trying to decide which ones to choose. They knew that Buckley would look for an all-white jury that would find Carl Lee guilty. They needed to get some black people on the jury – but they also knew it would be difficult because there were so few blacks in Clanton. The second job was to prepare Carl Lee's insanity defense. This was Ellen's responsibility.

By the end of the week, Jake knew the names and life histories

*National Guard: the part of the army that is responsible for peace-keeping inside the US.

of every person on the jury list, and Ellen had given him a thick file which contained everything he needed to present a strong insanity defense. He knew that he should feel confident, but he became more and more nervous as the first day of the trial came nearer.

Maybe it was the burning crosses that the Klan had put outside the houses of twenty of the people whose names were on the jury list. Maybe it was the late nights he was spending with Lucien, Harry Rex, and Ellen — and the large amounts of alcohol they all seemed to be drinking. Maybe it was just the fact that this was the biggest, most important trial he had ever worked on, that he had very little money, that his wife and daughter had had to leave town, and that his wife was still not speaking to him.

♦

On the morning of Monday, July 22, the day they were going to choose the jury, Jake woke up in his office before the sun, feeling terrible after another late night and too much whiskey. Harry Rex came early with breakfast. Jake could not eat his, so Harry Rex ate for the two of them. Ellen arrived a little later, dressed in a dark gray suit. Harry Rex told her that it was the first time she looked like a lawyer.

As the sun rose, the National Guard started to move around the court building. Soldiers stood at each corner of the courthouse square, watching the groups of reporters, black people, and Klan members who had started to arrive. As soon as they saw the white masks, the black people started to shout: "Free Carl Lee! Free Carl Lee!"

The Klan replied by screaming back, "Fry Carl Lee! Fry Carl Lee!"

Soldiers carrying guns ran across the square and stood between the two groups.

By the time the buses carrying the possible jury members arrived, Jake felt terrible. When he was still a young lawyer, Lucien had told him to make friends with fear because it would never go away. Lucien had also said that the jury always listened to a lawyer who was brave enough to be himself. Jake knew about the fear, but was not sure if he wanted to be himself – his head ached too much.

"How are you, boss?" Ellen asked.

"Ready, I guess. We'll leave in a minute."

"There are some reporters waiting outside. I told them you had dropped the case and left town."

"Wouldn't that be nice?"

◆

Jury selection was a long and complicated process. One hundred and fourteen people had been asked to do their duty as citizens. The twenty who had had a burning cross in their yards were told that they need not stay. That left ninety-four names.

Each lawyer then had the right to interview each juror. Buckley began with a list of a thousand questions. When Noose stopped him at five o'clock, he had still not finished. He said he would finish in the morning.

◆

The next day the sun rose quickly. A morning mist hung over the ground, wetting the boots of the soldiers outside the courthouse. By the time breakfast was served, the day was already hot and the soldiers had taken off their jackets and stood around in their pale green undershirts.

The black church leaders and their followers returned to their part of the square, and the Klansmen kept together on their side. It was 9 a.m. of Day Two.

Jake had a difficult job to do after Buckley's three-hour questioning the day before. His first question showed that he wanted to simplify things.

"Ladies and gentlemen. Do any of you believe that the insanity defense should not be used in a murder trial?"

The possible jurors looked at each other, but no hands went up. Insanity! Insanity! The seed had been planted.

"If we prove that Carl Lee Hailey was legally insane when he shot Billy Ray Cobb and Pete Willard, is there a person here who cannot find him not guilty?"

The question was hard to follow – that was the way Jake wanted it. Again there were no hands. A few wanted to answer, but they were not sure how to.

Jake looked at them carefully. He knew that most of them were confused, but he also knew that for this moment every possible juror was thinking about his client being insane. He would leave them there.

"Thank you," he said with all the charm he could manage. "I have no more questions."

Buckley looked confused. He stared at the judge.

"Is that all?" Noose asked. "Is that all Mr. Brigance?"

"Yes, sir. These citizens look fine to me," Jake said. The group was not at all acceptable to Jake – too white, too many women – but there was no sense repeating the same questions Buckley had asked.

Now that the list of possible jurors had been agreed, the next stage of jury selection could begin. Judge Noose and the lawyers left the courtroom and sat at the table in the judge's office. Noose looked at his numbered list and then looked at his lawyers.

"Gentlemen, are you ready? Good. Since this is a murder case, each of you has the right to refuse to accept twelve of the jurors. Mr. Buckley, you must now give a list of twelve jurors to the defense. Please start with juror Number One and refer to each juror only by number."

As they worked through the selection process, it became clear that Jake's worst fears were coming true. Buckley repeatedly suggested white jurors who were clearly against Carl Lee. Jake could not say no to them all – twelve was the limit – so he found himself accepting people he knew would be against his client. And each time Jake offered one of the few jurors he really wanted, Buckley refused him or her. The numbers were on Buckley's side. For every juror that Jake thought might be good for Carl Lee, Buckley had ten who would be against him.

When the last juror had been chosen, Judge Noose and the lawyers returned to their places. His Honor called the names of the twelve and they slowly, nervously made their way to the jury box. Ten women, two men, all white. The blacks in the courtroom looked at each other in disbelief.

"Did you pick that jury?" Carl Lee asked Jake.

♦

Stump Sisson died on Tuesday night at the burns hospital in Memphis. Four people had now died as a result of the rape of Tonya Hailey: Cobb, Willard, Bud Twitty, and now Sisson. When the Klan members met in the woods that evening, they wanted revenge. Stump Sisson would be remembered.

♦

Around midnight, Jake walked up and down his office and gave his opening speech for the hundredth time. Ellen listened. She had listened, objected, criticized, and argued for two hours. She was tired now. He did it perfectly. When he finished they went to the window and watched the lights being held by the blacks sitting in the darkness of the square.

They could hear laughter from the card games in the soldiers' tents. There was no moon.

Chapter 11   The Trial Begins

The bus arrived at the courthouse five minutes before nine. The jurors looked out through darkened windows to see how many blacks and how many Klansmen were waiting – and how many National Guard soldiers. When Judge Noose was ready to start, they were led into the courtroom and then into the jury box.

Rufus Buckley, as prosecutor, had the right to speak first, and he clearly intended to enjoy every minute. He started by thanking the jurors for being there (as if they had a choice, thought Jake). He said he was proud to be working with them in this most important case.

Jake sat and listened. It was all garbage and he had heard it before, but it still annoyed him because the jury sometimes believed it. Then Buckley started to talk about the rape and how terrible it was. He said that he was a father too – in fact he had a daughter the same age as Tonya Hailey – but that no one could take the law into their own hands.

Jake smiled quickly at Ellen. This was interesting. Buckley had chosen to talk about the rape instead of keeping it from the jury. Jake had been expecting a problem with Buckley when it came to this topic. Normally it would not be accepted as evidence during a murder trial – especially the more unpleasant details. But now Buckley had introduced the subject, so he was not going to be able to object when Jake told the jury about what the murdered men had done, and how the rape had destroyed Tonya's life – and the life of Carl Lee Hailey.

The next mistake that Buckley made was to speak for too

long. Although he had started with the jury on his side, by the end they were bored and finding it difficult to stay awake. Jake was winning the first argument without saying a word.

Jake had already planned a short opening speech, and after Buckley's effort he decided to make it even shorter. He only spoke for fourteen minutes, and the jury liked every word. He began by talking about daughters and how special they are. He told them about his own daughter and the special relationship that exists between father and daughter. He started to tell them how he would feel if she was raped by two drunk, drugged animals who tied her to a tree and . . .

"Objection," shouted Buckley.

"Sustained," Noose shouted back.

Jake ignored the shouting and continued softly. He asked the jury to try to imagine, through the whole trial, how they would feel if it was their daughter. He asked them not to find Carl Lee guilty, but to send him home to his family. He didn't talk about insanity yet. They knew it was coming. He finished shortly after he started, and left the jury with a strong sense of the difference between the two lawyers.

"Is that all?" Noose asked in surprise. "Well then, Mr. Buckley. You may call your first witness."

"The State calls Nora Cobb."

The mother of the murdered rapist sat in the witness box and listened to Rufus Buckley as he asked her where she lived, and what had happened on the day her son, Billy Ray Cobb, was killed. As Nora Cobb told her story, she started to cry.

She was not a witness who could do much damage to Carl Lee, and normally Jake would not ask her any questions. But then he saw an opportunity he could not miss – he could wake up Judge Noose and start making the jury think about what people like Billy Ray Cobb were really like. He also felt that Nora

Cobb's tears were the result of good acting – not deep regret.

"Just a few questions," Jake said as he stood up. "Mrs. Cobb, is it true that your son sold drugs?"

"Objection!" Buckley shouted, jumping to his feet. "The criminal record of the victim cannot be mentioned in court!"

"Sustained!"

Mrs. Cobb wiped her eyes and started to cry harder.

"You say your son was twenty-three when he died. In his twenty-three years, how many other children did he rape?"

"Objection! Objection!" shouted Buckley again, waving his arms and looking desperately at Judge Noose.

"Sustained! Sustained! Mr. Brigance! You cannot ask these questions!"

Mrs. Cobb burst into tears and the sound of her crying filled the shocked courtroom. But Jake had made his point. The jury would now remember the sort of man Billy Ray Cobb had been.

The next witness was Earnestine Willard, the mother of the other victim. She was less of an actress than Mrs. Cobb, but Rufus Buckley asked her the same questions he had asked the first witness, and brought the same tears to her eyes. When he had finished, Jake stood up.

"Mrs. Willard, I'm Jake Brigance." He stood in front of her and looked at her without pity. "How old was your son when he died?"

"Twenty-seven."

Buckley pushed his chair from the table and sat on its edge, ready to jump up. Noose removed his glasses and leaned forward.

"During his twenty-seven years, how many other children did he rape?"

Buckley immediately shouted, "Objection! Objection! Objection!"

"Sustained! Sustained! Sustained!"

The shouting frightened Mrs. Willard, and she cried louder. But once again, Jake had made his point.

♦

Ozzie was the first State witness after lunch. Buckley questioned him first, asking him to repeat exactly what had happened on the day of the murder. He then showed Ozzie the gun that Carl Lee had used, and asked him to say if this was the one he had found near the bodies. To finish, he then brought out a set of color photographs of the murder victims, some taken so close you could see how the bullets had broken through the skin and bone. Rufus Buckley made the jury members look at each picture, pointing out the horror of the way the two men had died. He wanted them to remember the violence of what Carl Lee had done.

♦

Jake looked at his notes as he walked across the courtroom. He had just a few questions for his friend.

"Sheriff, did you put Billy Ray Cobb and Pete Willard in jail?"

"Yes I did," answered the sheriff.

"For what reason?"

"For the rape of Tonya Hailey."

"And how old was she at the time of the rape?"

"She was ten."

"Is it true, Sheriff, that Pete Willard signed a written document saying that he had raped Tonya Hailey?"

"Objection! Objection! Your Honor! We can't discuss this case and Mr. Brigance knows it."

Ozzie had already said yes.

"Sustained."

"Please ignore the last question from Mr. Brigance," Noose told the jury.

"No further questions," said Jake.

♦

The next two witnesses gave technical evidence to show that Carl Lee Hailey had, as everyone knew, killed Cobb and Willard. Again Buckley bored the jury by going into great detail and asking long and complicated questions. The jury members were becoming increasingly tired of the sound of his voice.

When it was Jake's turn to ask questions, he said that he had none.

♦

The second day of the trial started in the same way, with the jurors in their seats by nine o'clock. Rufus Buckley brought in his next witness, the doctor who had examined Cobb and Willard's bodies. Again, Buckley talked too long and asked too many questions. No one was denying that Cobb and Willard had been killed with an M-16, or that Carl Lee had killed them, so why spend so much time on it? The jury members were bored and the judge spent a lot of time cleaning his glasses in order to stay awake.

Once again, when it came to Jake's turn, he looked at the judge and said, "I have no questions." Judge Noose and the jurors all smiled. It was becoming clear which lawyer they preferred, but Buckley still didn't seem to understand what he was doing wrong.

The last witness was Officer DeWayne Looney. Buckley had chosen him to speak last as a way of reminding the jury of the damage Carl Lee had done. Looney walked into the courtroom with difficulty, leaning on a stick.

Buckley asked Deputy Looney his age, where he worked, and

who he took to the courthouse on Monday, May 20. He then asked what had happened when he had taken the men out of the court. Deputy Looney described how he had led the prisoners out of the court and how, suddenly, Carl Lee had come out of a side room.

"Then what happened?" asked Buckley.

"When Cobb was near to the foot of the stairs, the shooting started. I was waiting to go on down. I didn't see anybody for a second, then I saw Mr. Hailey with the machine gun. Cobb was blown backward into Willard, and they both screamed and fell down, trying to get back up to where I was."

"Yes, sir. Please describe what you saw."

"You could hear the bullets coming off the walls and hitting everywhere. It was the loudest gun I ever heard."

"What happened to you?"

"I never got down the stairs. I think one of the bullets came off the wall and caught me in the leg."

"And what happened to your leg?"

"They cut it off," he answered softly. "Just below the knee."

"Did you get a good look at the man with the gun?"

"Yes, sir. It was Mr. Hailey, the man sitting over there."

That answer was a good place to stop asking questions. But Buckley then took out large plans of the courthouse and arranged them in front of the jury so that Looney could walk around and show his bad leg. Jake rubbed his forehead and Noose cleaned and re-cleaned his glasses. The jurors moved around in their chairs. Buckley had lost them again.

"Any questions, Mr. Brigance?" Noose asked at last.

"Just a few questions. Officer Looney, who was Carl Lee looking at when he was shooting?"

"Those boys, I think."

"Did he ever look at you?"

"I don't think so."

"So he didn't aim the gun at you?"

"Oh no, sir. He just aimed at those boys. Hit them too."

"What did he do when he was shooting?"

"He just screamed and laughed like a crazy man. It was the strangest thing I ever heard. With all the noise, the gun firing, the bullets whistling, the boys screaming as they got hit – over all that noise I could hear him laughing that crazy laugh. That's what I'll always remember."

The answer was so perfect that Jake had to fight off a smile. He and Looney had worked on it a hundred times, and it was a thing of beauty. Every word was perfect. Jake looked through his notes and then looked up at the jurors. They were all waiting for the next question. Jake wrote something down and then looked carefully at Looney, just to make the silence last a few more seconds.

"Now, Deputy Looney, Carl Lee Hailey shot you in the leg."

"Yes sir, he did."

"Do you think he meant to?"

"No sir. It was an accident. I do not want to see him punished for the shooting, sir. I have no bad feelings about the man. I would do the same."

Buckley dropped his pen and sat back in his chair. He looked sadly at his star witness.

"What do you mean by that?" Jake asked.

"I mean I don't blame him for what he did. Those boys raped his little girl. I've got a little girl. If somebody raped her, I'd kill him just like Carl Lee did. We should give him a prize!"

"Do you want the jury to find Carl Lee guilty?"

Buckley jumped and shouted, "Objection! He can't ask that question!"

"No," Looney shouted. "I don't want him to be found guilty. He's a hero."

"Don't answer, Mr. Looney," Noose said loudly. "Don't answer!"

"He's a hero! Set him free!" Looney shouted at Buckley.

"Order! Order!" Noose banged his table.

Buckley was silent. Looney was silent. Jake walked to his chair and said he had no other questions. Looney smiled at the jury and walked slowly and painfully from the courtroom.

Chapter 12   A Crazy World

Jake awoke in the darkness to the sound of his doorbell. He opened the front door in his nightshirt and found Ozzie and Deputy Nesbit waiting for him.

"What is it?" he asked as he opened the door.

"They're going to kill you today," Ozzie said.

"Who?"

"The Klan."

"How do you know?"

"The same man who told us about the dynamite – he calls himself Mickey Mouse. He telephoned yesterday and said you're the lucky man. Today is the big day. That's why we're here. We're coming to the office with you. We're staying with you all day."

At five-thirty, they drove Jake to his office and locked the door. At eight, a group of soldiers was waiting on the sidewalk. Harry Rex and Ellen watched from the second floor of the courthouse. Jake walked between Ozzie and Nesbit, the three of them in the middle of the group of soldiers.

The Klan's man sat with his gun in his hands at a window in an old, empty factory two blocks north and east of the square. From his position he had a clear view of the back of the courthouse. He sat in the darkness and aimed through a small opening, knowing that no one in the world could see him. Another Klan member waited in a pickup down the road. The engine was running and the driver sat smoking, waiting for the sound of the gun.

When he saw the group of soldiers move away from Jake's office, the gunman did not know what to do. He could only see the top of Jake's head in a sea of green army hats. He could not be sure of hitting Jake, but the whiskey he had been drinking made him want some excitement. He aimed and fired, hoping for the best.

When they heard the sound of the gun the soldiers ran toward the courthouse, pulling Jake down with them. One soldier screamed in pain, holding his throat. Another shot. Then another.

"He's hit!" someone shouted. Jake ran through the doors to the safety of the building. He fell onto the floor and put his head in his hands. Ozzie stood next to him, watching the soldiers through the door.

The gunman ran out of the factory and threw his weapon behind the back seat of the pickup. The two men drove out of town. They were going to a funeral in south Mississippi.

♦

The soldier had been standing by Jake's left shoulder when he was hit.

"This is kind of silly, ain't it?" he had just said to Jake when the bullet shot through his throat. He fell against Jake, holding his neck, losing blood fast and screaming.

"He's dead, isn't he!" Jake asked Ozzie softly. "He's dead. I know he's dead. I heard his neck break."

They heard later that the soldier did not die, but he was not going to be able to walk again. Jake managed, with difficulty, to persuade the judge that the trial could wait for another twenty-four hours. He stayed in the office with Harry Rex and Ellen

Roark. After he had phoned his wife to tell her he was unhurt, he sat with his friends, talking too much and drinking too much. Dr. Bass joined them later in the day, and then Lester Hailey arrived with Lucien. Lucien bought more drinks and, by the end of the afternoon, Jake was drunk enough to fall asleep on the floor. Ellen slept on the sofa in Jake's office.

◆

When Ellen woke up, the room was dark and empty and smelled of alcohol. She moved around carefully and found her boss peacefully sleeping on the floor in the conference room. It was ten o'clock. She had slept five hours. She could stay at Lucien's house, but needed to change clothes. She locked the front door and walked to her car.

Ellen had almost arrived at Oxford when she saw the blue lights behind her. As usual, she was driving at seventy-five miles an hour. She parked at the side of the road, got out of the car and waited for the police.

Two men approached from the blue lights. Suddenly, she was knocked to the ground. A heavy blanket was thrown over her and both men held her down. A rope was tied around her chest and waist. She kicked and swore, but could do little to help herself.

One of them removed her keys from the car and opened the trunk. They threw her inside and banged it shut. One of the men then took the blue lights off their car and drove away, followed by the other in Ellen's BMW. They found a side road and followed it deep into the woods, then turned off the road into a small field where a large cross was being burned by a number of Ku Klux Klan members.

The two men quickly put on their white robes and masks. They pulled her out of the trunk and threw her to the ground. They tied her arms and legs, placed a cloth over her mouth and dragged her to a large pole a few feet from the cross. They tied her to the pole with her back to the Klan members.

The burning cross lit the field. As the heat from the fire started to burn her, she struggled with the ropes but she couldn't loosen them. She started to make strange crying noises deep in her throat.

A masked figure left the others and approached her. She could hear his footsteps and then felt his breath on her face.

"You nigger-lover," he said in an educated mid-western voice. He pulled the collar of her shirt and tore it from her back. He pulled down the zipper on her skirt and then took out a large knife, cut the skirt and underclothes from top to bottom, and pulled them from around her. She tried to kick, but the heavy rope around her ankles held her feet to the pole.

"See what happens to nigger-lovers," he said quietly. "How do you like it?"

The fire was hot now. Her red hair was wet around her neck and shoulders. One of the others handed the man a long whip. He moved it up and down quickly, making it crack. Then he walked backward, carefully measuring the distance to the pole.

He brought the whip up in the air and aimed at her back, but the tallest Klan leader stepped forward and raised his hand to stop the arm from coming down. Nothing was said, but the whip was put away.

The man walked back to her and cut her hair with his knife until the skin of her head could be seen, ugly and bleeding. She made quiet crying sounds, but did not move.

The Klan members moved away to their cars. A can of gasoline was poured inside the BMW with Massachusetts numbers and somebody threw a match. The car burned very quickly.

When he was certain they were gone, the man Ozzie called Mickey Mouse came out from the bushes. He untied her and carried her away from the field. He tried to cover her with what was left of her clothes. He then drove to Oxford to a pay phone, and called the county sheriff.

◆

Jake woke with another headache, but he knew that he had to go to court and face the world again. When he got into court, Judge Noose asked him how he was feeling. He said he felt better than the soldier who got hit.

Jake's first witness was the psychiatrist, Dr. W.T. Bass. Jake was pleased that he did not look drunk. He looked good, in an expensive suit and white shirt. He even sounded good as Jake led him through a long series of questions about his qualifications and his experience as a psychiatrist.

Then Buckley got up to ask some questions. He asked how many books Dr. Bass had written. None. He asked how many hospitals he worked in. None. He asked how many patients the doctor saw. A few. As the questions continued, Dr. Bass began to look less good and Jake felt more worried.

Jake returned to the list of questions in his note book. He asked Dr. Bass when and how often he had examined Carl Lee Hailey. He asked about Carl Lee's experience in Vietnam, and the effect it had had on him. Carl Lee listened carefully – the doctor was sounding good again. Jake then asked him about the rape, and Dr. Bass explained how Carl Lee had been unbalanced by the rape, how he had stopped being himself. Then, when he visited his daughter in hospital, she told him how she had called for him in the woods. She thought she saw him, but he didn't come. She continued calling, but the men told her she had no father now.

Dr. Bass then answered questions about the insanity defense and the M'Naghten Rule on which it was based. Bass explained

63

that the rule went back to England in 1843, when Daniel M'Naghten tried to kill a politician called Sir Robert Peel. He did not succeed but accidentally shot and killed the politician's secretary. During his trial it became clear that M'Naghten was insane and the jury decided that he was not guilty by reason of insanity. From this the M'Naghten Rule was made, and it is still followed in England and sixteen US states.

"What does the M'Naghten Rule really mean?" Jake asked.

"Well, it's fairly simple. To use insanity as a defense you must prove that the person did what he or she did because they had a mental disease or that they did not know the nature and quality of what they were doing."

"Can you simplify that?"

"Yes. If someone cannot tell the difference between right and wrong, he or she is legally insane. This is what happened to Carl Lee Hailey. After the rape he expected someone to kill the rapists. He couldn't understand why it did not happen. He didn't know what else to do. He had to kill them."

Jake let the jury think about these words.

"Now, Dr. Bass, do you have an opinion, to a reasonable degree of medical certainty, whether Carl Lee Hailey was able to know the difference between right and wrong when he shot these men?"

"I have."

"And what is that opinion?"

"Because of his mental condition, he was unable to tell right from wrong."

"Thank you, Doctor."

Jake picked up his note book and walked back to his seat. He looked at Lucien, who was smiling, and at the jury. They were watching Bass and thinking about what he had said. Wanda Wornack, a young kind-looking woman, looked at Jake and smiled. It was the most positive signal he had received from the jury since the trial started.

"Pretty good," Carl Lee said quietly.

♦

Judge Noose asked Buckley if he had any questions.

"Just a few," Buckley said as he walked to the front of the courtroom. "Dr. Bass, what is your full name?"

Jake froze. There was something wrong about the question.

"William Tyler Bass."

"What name are you generally known by?"

"W.T. Bass."

"Have you ever been known as Tyler Bass?"

The medical witness hesitated.

"No," he said.

Jake felt a sudden fear in his stomach. The question could only mean trouble.

"You're telling this jury that on October 17, 1956, in Dallas, Texas, you were not found guilty of a crime under the name of Tyler Bass?"

"That's a lie," Bass said quietly.

"Are you sure it's a lie?" Buckley asked. "Do you know a lie from the truth, Dr. Bass? Do you know the difference between right and wrong? Because, Dr. Bass, I've got some photographs of you taken by the Dallas Police Department on September 11, 1956, when you were charged with the rape of a 17-year-old girl."

The silence in the room was complete. W.T. Bass could only look at the ground. He knew that there was nothing he could say. No one would believe him.

"We have no further questions for the defense's medical witness," Buckley said.

A speech was needed. A brilliant, emotional explanation that would touch the hearts of the jurors and make them cry with pity for Bass and for Carl Lee. But Jake could think of nothing to say. He wanted to be sick. Everything had fallen to pieces. Buckley had destroyed his medical witness and had destroyed the insanity defense he had tried to build. And it was all Jake's fault. He thought he was so clever, he thought he would win, and he had chosen a medical witness who was a drunk and a rapist. Nothing could help Carl Lee now. Dr. Bass walked out of the courtroom, but no one watched him go.

"Mr. Brigance, you may call your next witness."

Jake tried to stand up but his legs felt like water. As he stood up, Ozzie came to his rescue. The sheriff approached the clerk of the court and gave him a message. The clerk handed this to the judge, who read it and then looked up and said that the court would take a break for an hour. He asked the lawyers to come to his office. As soon as they were in the room, Ozzie turned and spoke to Jake.

"Jake, I have some bad news. I got a call an hour ago from the sheriff of Lafayette County. Your law clerk, Ellen Roark, is in hospital."

Jake had thought that things could not get worse. It seemed that they could.

"What happened?"

"The Klan got her last night. Somewhere between here and Oxford. They tied her to a tree."

"How is she?" Jake asked.

"She'll be OK."

"What happened?" Buckley asked.

"We ain't sure. They stopped her car somehow and took her out in the woods. Cut her clothes off her and cut her hair. She's got cuts on the head, so they think she was beaten."

Jake needed to be sick. He couldn't speak. The judge looked at him and said they'd better take a break until two o'clock.

♦

At the end of the afternoon, Jake walked slowly up the front steps to his office. He wanted to kill W. T. Bass, to break the head of the so-called friend who had introduced him to the drunk psychiatrist. Lucien was there, holding a drink. They said nothing. Lucien looked away. Then he spoke in an unusually quiet voice.

"You should know that according to Bass the girl was seventeen and the daughter of a judge in Dallas. They fell in love but got caught on the judge's sofa. The judge had big political connections and got Bass arrested for rape. But they were in love, so before he got put in prison he married her. She had a perfect baby boy – the first grandchild. The judge dropped the rape charge, and Bass didn't have to go to prison."

Lucien drank and watched the lights from the square.

"What happened to the girl?" asked Jake.

"According to Bass, a week before he finished medical school, his wife and the little boy were killed in a train accident in Fort Worth. That's when he started drinking, and stopped living."

Jake looked out of the window. There was nothing to say.

"How's Row Ark?" Lucien asked.

"They say she'll be OK. I called her room and a nurse said she couldn't talk. I'll go over tomorrow."

"I hope she's OK. She's a fine girl," said Lucien.

"I feel like it's my fault, Lucien."

"It's not your fault. It's a crazy world, Jake. Full of crazy people. Right now I think half of them are in Ford County."

♦

Jake stayed at the office that night, talking to Lucien. He fell asleep on the sofa, but was woken at midnight by Deputy Nesbit shouting: "Get up, Jake! You've got to go home! It's an emergency!"

Jake jumped to his feet and followed Nesbit. Adams Street was blocked by fire-engines parked in front of Jake's house. The firefighters worked desperately, directing jets of water at the center of the fire. Jake saw Ozzie standing near a police car with the fire chief.

The fire was brilliant. Flames came from every window across the front of the house, upstairs and down. At the side of the house, Carla's car burned inside and out. After watching for a minute or two as the water disappeared into the flames with no noticeable effect, the fire chief said, "It'll burn to the ground." The Klan had done a good job. After Bass and Ellen Roark, Jake thought he had hit the bottom. Now he began to think there was no bottom.

Jake turned to Deputy Nesbit. "Will you do something for me?"

"Sure, Jake."

"Drive over to Harry Rex's and bring him back. I'd hate him to miss this."

"Sure."

For two hours Jake, Ozzie, Harry Rex, and Nesbit sat on the police car and watched the fire burn. It burned until morning. As the sun began to appear, Jake thanked the firefighters. He and Harry Rex walked through the back yard and looked at the damage.

"Oh well," Harry Rex said. "It's just a house."

"Would you call Carla and tell her that?"

"No. I think *you* should."

"I think I'll wait."

Harry Rex looked at his watch. "It's about breakfast time, isn't it?"

"It's Sunday morning, Harry Rex. Nothing's open."

"Ah, Jake, I'm a professional. I can find hot food at any time of any day."

"The truck stop?"

"The truck stop!"

"OK. And when we finish we'll go to Oxford to check on Row Ark."

Chapter 13   The Trial Ends

Clanton returned to normal Monday morning as the crowd of blacks and whites gathered in the square. The soldiers were there to keep the peace. The Klan were louder than ever. They had begun to think they might win, and were pleased with the direct hit on Jake's house.

Jake felt lonely walking into the court without Ellen. He and Harry Rex had been to see her at the hospital, and she was going to be OK. She had been badly frightened, but now she was angry and desperately wanted Jake to win. He did too, but did not feel so confident. He could still remember how sick he had felt, and how he could not find anything to say when Buckley had destroyed Dr. Bass.

"Does the State have any final witness?" Judge Noose asked Rufus Buckley.

"One witness, Your Honor."

Dr. Rodeheaver sat carefully in the witness chair and looked at the jury. He looked like a real psychiatrist. Dark suit, no cowboy boots.

Buckley stood and smiled at the jury.

69

"You are Dr. Wilbert Rodeheaver?"

"I am," he replied.

Buckley asked the doctor questions, a million questions, about his educational and professional background. Rodeheaver was confident, relaxed, prepared, and he was used to being in the witness chair. He gave good answers.

Jake had no questions.

Buckley then asked Dr. Rodeheaver to describe his examination of Carl Lee Hailey. Dr. Rodeheaver said that Carl Lee was fairly helpful and able to talk about his experience in Vietnam and his family, but said that he was unable to remember details of the day of the murder. The doctor talked about the number of times he had met Carl Lee and the questions he had asked. He said that it was his opinion that Mr. Hailey had carefully planned what he did and he knew what he was doing."

"Did you know," asked Buckley, "that another psychiatrist, a Dr. W.T. Bass, has told this jury that Mr. Hailey was unable to recognize the difference between right and wrong, and that he was insane when he murdered these two men?"

"Yes, I did know that."

"Do you agree with that opinion?"

"No, I do not, and I do not find it professionally acceptable. Mr. Hailey himself has said that he planned the murders. By saying this he has shown that he was not insane. He knew what he was doing, and he knew right from wrong."

"Doctor, what, therefore, is your medical opinion of the mental condition of Mr. Hailey on the day he shot Billy Ray Cobb, Peter Willard, and Deputy DeWayne Looney?"

"His mental condition was normal, and he could tell right from wrong."

"Thank you, Doctor. I have no further questions."

"Any questions, Mr. Brigance?" Noose asked.

"A few questions, Your Honor."

Working from his notes, Jake asked Dr. Rodeheaver a series of careful questions about the theory of psychiatry. The doctor agreed that psychiatry could never be an exact science, and that there would always be different opinions.

Jake then asked how many cases Dr. Rodeheaver had been a witness in. He replied that this was the forty-third.

Jake checked something in a file and looked at the doctor with a nasty little smile.

"Are you sure it's not your forty-sixth?"

"It could be, yes. I'm not certain."

The courtroom became still. Buckley looked up from his notes and watched his witness carefully.

"Forty-six times you've spoken for the State in insanity trials?"

"If you say so."

"And forty-six times you've said that the defendant was not legally insane. Correct, Doctor?"

"I'm not sure."

"Well, let me make it simple. You've been a witness forty-six times, and forty-six times it has been your opinion the defendant was not legally insane. Correct?"

Rodeheaver moved in his chair and, for the first time, looked uncomfortable.

"I'm not sure."

"You've never seen a legally insane defendant, have you, Doctor?"

"Of course I have."

"Good. Would you then, please sir, tell us the name of the defendant and where he was tried?"

Rodeheaver breathed deeply and looked at the ceiling. Jake looked across at the jurors. They were awake and waiting for an answer.

"I can't remember," he finally said.

Jake lifted a pile of papers and waved it at the witness.

"Is it possible, Doctor, that the reason you can't remember is that in eleven years, forty-six trials, you have never spoken *for* the defendant?"

"I honestly can't remember."

"Can you honestly name us one trial in which you found the defendant to be legally insane?"

"I'm sure there are some."

"Yes or no, Doctor. One trial?"

The medical witness looked at Buckley.

"No, my memory fails me. I cannot."

Jake walked slowly to the defense table and picked up a thick file.

"Dr. Rodeheaver, do you remember being a witness in the trial of a man by the name of Danny Booker in McMurphy County in December 1975?"

"Yes, I remember that trial."

"And you said that he was not legally insane, didn't you?"

"That is correct."

"Do you remember how many psychiatrists spoke for him?"

"Not exactly. There were several."

"There were three, Dr. Rodeheaver, and they all said the man was legally insane. How many other doctors agreed with you?"

"None, if I remember correctly."

"So it was three against one."

"Yes, but . . ."

"What did the jury do, Doctor?"

"He was found not guilty by reason of insanity."

"Thank you. Now, Dr. Rodeheaver, you're the head doctor at Whitfield Psychiatric Hospital, aren't you?"

"Yes."

"And where is Danny Booker today?"

Rodeheaver looked desperately at Buckley but then had to turn back to Jake to answer the question. He waited one second too long for the jury. They were losing trust in him.

"He's at Whitfield, isn't he?" Jake asked.

"I believe so," Rodeheaver said.

"And is this man legally insane, Doctor?"

"I don't think so."

"But you said in court that Danny Booker was not mad and understood what he was doing when he killed his wife. The jury disagreed with you and found him not guilty, and since that time he has been a patient in your hospital, under your care, and treated as a patient with a mental illness. Is that correct?"

The jury could see that it was.

And Jake then asked the doctor about five more cases – four men and one woman. In each one Dr. Rodeheaver had said the person was not insane, but in each case the jury had disagreed – and now they were all in Dr. Rodeheaver's hospital. Jake asked how this was possible.

"You just can't trust juries," said the doctor, without thinking. Jake looked at him with a sad smile, then looked at the jury. He folded his arms and allowed Rodeheaver's words to sink in. He waited, looking at the witness. Finally he turned to the judge.

"I think we've heard enough from this witness, Your Honor. We have no more questions."

Jake knew that he had destroyed Buckley's medical witness. There were no more witnesses. It was time for the closing arguments.

◆

Jake talked directly to the jury. He began with his biggest problem, Dr. W. T. Bass. He apologized to the jury. He asked them to believe that he would never use a man with a criminal record as a witness if he knew the facts. He raised his hand and swore to them that he had not known.

He then asked them to think about what Dr. Bass had said. Yes, thirty years ago he had had sex with a girl under eighteen in Texas. Does that mean he is lying now in this trial? Does that mean you cannot trust his professional opinion?

"Be fair to Bass the psychiatrist. Forget Bass the person. And please be fair to his patient, Carl Lee Hailey. He knew nothing of the doctor's past."

Then Jake told them that the girl had become Bass's wife and had died with their child in a train crash. Mr. Buckley had not mentioned that. He waited a moment and let them think about it.

"And what about Dr. Rodeheaver?" he asked. "Maybe he had sex with a girl under eighteen once, maybe he didn't. Does that make him a better or a worse psychiatrist? The problem with Dr. Rodeheaver is that although he is a highly trained doctor who treats thousands of people for all sorts of mental illnesses, when crimes are involved he cannot recognize insanity."

They watched him, listened to every word. He was not loud and over-confident like Buckley. He was quiet. He looked tired, almost hurt.

Jake asked the jury to forgive him for his lack of experience. If he had made mistakes, it was not his client's fault.

He talked about daughters. He told the jury about his own daughter. She was four, almost five, and she was the center of his world. She was special, she was a little girl, and he had to protect her.

Carl Lee had a daughter. Her name was Tonya. He pointed to her on the front row next to her mother and brothers.

"She's a beautiful little girl, ten years old. And now she can never have children. She can never have a daughter . . ."

"Objection!" Buckley shouted.

"Sustained."

Jake talked about rape, and explained how rape is much worse than murder. With murder, the victim is gone, and not forced to deal with what happened to her. The family must deal with it, but not the victim. But rape is much worse. The victim has a lifetime of trying to understand, of asking questions, and knowing the rapist may someday escape or be freed. Every hour of every day, the victim thinks of the rape and asks herself a thousand questions. She relives it, step by step, minute by minute, and it hurts just as badly.

And if this happens to a child? A ten-year-old child?

Imagine you're a parent. How would you explain to your child why she was raped? How would you explain why she cannot have children?

"Objection."

"Sustained. Please ignore that, ladies and gentlemen."

"What would you do?" asked Jake. "What would a father do?"

Jake paused for a drink of water. He changed direction now. He stopped looking hurt. He looked angry. He talked about Cobb and Willard. Drug sellers and rapists. Was this country a better place without them? Certainly – and Deputy Looney, a man who had lost a leg, thought so too. He had said that they should thank Carl Lee for what he had done. He was a hero. He asked the jury to follow Looney's wishes.

He became much quieter, and said he was almost finished. He wanted to leave them with one thought. Picture this if they could. "When she was lying there, beaten, covered in her own blood, tied to two trees, she had looked into the woods around her. She wanted her daddy. She thought he was coming but it was only a dream."

"Ladies and gentlemen," he continued. "She needs him now, as much as she needed him then. Please don't take him away. She's waiting on the front row for her daddy. Let him go home to his family."

The courtroom was silent as Jake sat down next to his client. He looked at the jury, and saw Wanda Wornack brush away a tear with her finger. For the first time in two days he felt some hope.

◆

At four o'clock, Judge Noose spoke to the jury. He told them to get organized, and get busy. He told them they could discuss things until six, maybe seven, but if they could not make a decision he would ask them to meet again on Tuesday morning. They stood up and walked out. No one expected a quick decision.

Chapter 14   Guilty or Not Guilty?

The jury did not make a decision by seven o'clock and Judge Noose instructed them to go back to their hotel and return to the court at 9 a.m. the next day. Jake went back to Lucien's house. He had no home, no wife, no law clerk, but at least he had some friends. Harry Rex joined them and they sat on the porch drinking beer and eating fried potatoes. They could only wait. Jake had done everything he could.

◆

At 9 a.m. the next day, the square in front of the courthouse was crowded again. Reverend Agee led his people as they shouted louder and louder, "Free Carl Lee! Free Carl Lee!" The Klan shouted back, "Fry Carl Lee!" but not as loudly as before. There seemed to be fewer of them today, and they did not seem so confident. Everyone had been talking about Jake's final speech.

The jury arrived and began their discussion in the jury room. Jake and Harry Rex sat in the empty courtroom looking across at Buckley. By midday, there was still no decision but the crowds outside the courthouse were getting bigger. During lunch the ten thousand grew to fifteen thousand.

Carl Lee had been allowed to come into the courtroom and sit with Tonya and the others. At four o'clock, around the time when the jury had to report to the judge, they walked to one of the tall windows at the front of the courtroom. Carl Lee noticed a small handle. He turned it, and the windows swung open. Carl Lee looked at the deputy beside him and stepped forward. He held Tonya in the air and watched the crowd.

They saw him. They shouted his name and rushed to the building under him. Reverend Agee led the marchers off the street and across the square. A wave of black people pressed forward for a closer look at their man.

"Free Carl Lee!"

"Free Carl Lee!"

"Free Carl Lee!"

He waved at his people below him. He kissed his daughter and his sons. He waved and told the children to wave too. The crowd went wild.

Judge Noose asked to see the lawyers in his office. He was worried. Buckley was angry and wanted a new trial. He said that the jury could not make a fair decision with this crowd outside.

Jake laughed at him, and said that he had wanted the trial to be moved away from Clanton. It was too late now. Buckley then said that the jury should be moved to another place while they made up their minds. Jake brought out a pile of legal documents which showed that this could not be done. They had to finish this business in Clanton.

When the jury came in to report, apart from the reporters, the courtroom was solid black. The Klan had clearly decided it was not a good place to be. The jurors looked tired and unhappy.

"Have you made a decision?" Judge Noose asked.

"No, sir," replied the head of the jury.

"Do you think you will be able to make a decision if you have more time?"

"We've talked about that, Your Honor. And we'd like to leave, get a good night's rest, and try again tomorrow. We're not ready to stop."

♦

Wednesday. For the first time in weeks, Jake slept more than eight hours. He had fallen asleep on the sofa in his office and he awoke at five to the sounds of the army getting ready for the worst. He had rested, but he could not stop thinking that this would probably be the big day. He showered and shaved downstairs. He then took a new shirt from its packet, and dressed himself in Lucien's best dark blue suit. It was too short and a bit loose, but not a bad fit under the circumstances. He thought about his house on Adams Street and how Carla would feel.

For the first time in a week, he went across to the Coffee Shop for breakfast. The manager, Dell, greeted him like a lost child and came and sat next to him at a corner table. As the other customers arrived and saw him, they stopped and shook his hand. It was good to see him again. They had missed him, and they were on his side. He looked thin, Dell said, so he ordered most of the things on the menu. It felt good to be there.

He stayed for an hour and talked to people, then went across to his office. There was nothing to do except wait. He sat by the window, drank coffee, smoked a cigarette, and watched the soldiers. He thought about a quiet little Southern law office with a secretary and clients waiting to see him. Of normal things, like a family, a home, and church on Sunday mornings. Maybe he should leave these big cases to others.

When the jury arrived at 9 a.m. as usual, there were even more people than the day before. The jurors could see nothing but a sea of black faces when their bus stopped outside the court. They were scared.

In the jury room, Wanda Wornack stood at the end of the table and nervously asked for attention.

"I have a suggestion," she said slowly, "that might help us decide this thing."

Suddenly she had their complete attention.

"I thought of something last night when I couldn't sleep, and I want you to think about it too. It may be painful. It may make you search your heart and take a long look at your soul. But I'll ask you to do it anyway. And if each of you will be honest with yourself, I think we can finish before midday."

The only sounds came from the street below.

"Good. This is what I want you to do. I want you to pretend with me for a moment. I want you to use your imaginations. I want you to close your eyes and listen to my voice and nothing else."

They closed their eyes. They were ready to try anything.

◆

At around eleven o'clock, the phone rang in Jake's office. It rang again, and Lucien answered it. He listened, then put the phone down.

"What is it?" Harry Rex demanded.

Jake sat up and looked at Lucien. The moment had arrived.

"The jury is ready."

"Oh my God," Jake said.

"Listen to me, Jake," said Lucien. "Stay calm. Be careful what you say."

"That's strange advice coming from you, Lucien," Jake replied.

"I've learned a lot. If you win, be careful what you say to reporters. Make sure you thank the jury. If you lose . . ."

"If you lose," Harry Rex said, "run as fast as you can, because those people out there will bring down the courthouse!"

"I feel weak," said Jake.

♦

When Jake entered the courtroom, Carl Lee was already there, sitting at the defense table. Gwen and Lester had tears in their eyes. The children were confused and scared.

Judge Noose came to his chair and sat down, and the courtroom became totally silent. There was no sound from the outside. Twenty thousand blacks knelt on the ground and prayed. There was perfect silence inside the courtroom and out.

The door from the jury room opened, and it seemed like an hour before the first juror came out with tears in her eyes. Jake dropped his head. Carl Lee looked ahead at a painting on the wall above Judge Noose's seat. The jurors slowly took their places. They seemed scared. Most had been crying. Jake felt sick. The head of the jury held a piece of paper.

"Ladies and gentlemen, have you made your decision?"

"Yes sir, we have," he answered quietly. His voice shook as he spoke.

"Hand it to the clerk, please."

She took it and handed it to His Honor, who studied it.

"It is technically in order," he finally said.

One juror was crying, the only sound in the courtroom. Other jurors held handkerchiefs to their eyes. The crying could mean only one thing to Jake.

Noose looked at Carl Lee.

"Will the defendant please rise."

Jake's client stood up slowly. Jake closed his eyes and stopped breathing. His hands shook and his stomach ached.

Noose handed the paper back to the clerk of the court.

"Please read it, Madam Clerk."

She unfolded it and faced the defendant.

"On each of the charges against him, we the jury find the defendant not guilty, by reason of insanity."

The courtroom exploded. Carl Lee turned and ran to where his children were sitting. Tonya and the boys reached forward and held him. Gwen screamed and burst into tears. She buried her head in Lester's arms. People stood on the seats and shouted "Praise the Lord!"

Jake felt nothing. His only movement was a weak smile in the direction of the jury. He wanted to cry, but just sat at the defense table trying to smile, unable to do anything else. From the corner of his eye he could see Buckley removing files and important-looking papers, and throwing them all into bags.

A boy ran between two deputies and out of the door, shouting "Not guilty! Not guilty!" to the crowd waiting outside.

Judge Noose looked at the lawyers. "If there is nothing else, this court will now close. As I have heard nothing to say that Mr. Hailey is now insane, he is free to leave this court."

Carl Lee stood in the middle of his family. They had their arms around him, and everyone was crying and shouting "Praise the Lord." They gathered round Jake and held him and said they loved him.

The reporters began firing questions at Jake. He held up his hands, and said he would make no comments now. But there would be a conference in his office at 2 p.m.

Buckley left through a side door. The jurors went back to the jury room to wait for the last bus ride to the hotel. The reporters crowded round Carl Lee.

"I just want to go home," he said again and again. "I just want to go home."

♦

After the dancing in the square outside the courthouse had ended, after the thousands of happy supporters had all gone home, Jake, Harry Rex, and Lucien went to Lucien's house and ate a mountain of pork and vegetables.

"You look very silly," Harry Rex said to Jake.

"Shut up, Harry Rex," Lucien said. "Let him enjoy his finest hour."

"He's enjoying it. Look at that smile."

"What should I tell reporters?" Jake asked.

"Tell them you need some clients," Harry Rex said.

"Clients will be no problem," Lucien said. "They'll be waiting on the sidewalks asking to meet you."

They drove back into town in Harry Rex's old Ford. As they passed a row of houses on the right, Jake asked him to stop. Harry Rex pulled off the road and parked under a tree. Jake got out, looked around the front yard, and walked onto the porch. He knocked on the door.

A man asked who was there.

"I'm Jake Brigance, and . . ."

The door flew open and the man came out and took Jake's hand.

"Nice to meet you, Jake. I'm Mack Loyd Crowell. You've done a good job. I'm proud to meet you."

Jake shook his hand.

"You looking for Wanda?" Crowell asked.

"Well, yes. I was just passing, and I remembered her address from the jury research."

"You've come to the right place. She lives here, and I do too most of the time. We ain't married, but we go together. She's lying down resting. She's pretty tired."

"Don't wake her," Jake said.

"She told me what happened. She won it for you."

"How? What happened?"

"She made them all close their eyes and listen to her. She told them to pretend that the little girl had blond hair and blue eyes, that the two rapists were black, that they tied her right foot to a tree and her left foot to a fence post, that they raped her repeatedly and swore at her because she was white. She told them to picture the little girl lying there, begging for her daddy while they kicked her in the mouth and knocked out her teeth, broke both jaws, broke her nose. She made them imagine two drunk blacks pouring beer on her like that and laughing. And then she told them to imagine that the little girl belonged to them – their daughter. She told them to be honest with themselves and to write on a piece of paper whether or not they would kill those men if they got the chance. And they voted on it. All twelve said they would do the killing. Twelve to zero. Wanda said she'd sit in that jury room until Christmas before she'd vote that Carl Lee was guilty, and if they were honest with themselves, then they ought to feel the same way. They agreed with her."

Jake listened to every word without breathing. He heard a noise. Wanda Wornack walked to the screen door. She smiled at him and began crying. He looked at her but could not talk. She wiped her eyes and looked at him, and shook the hand he held out to her.

◆

A hundred cars were parked east and west of the Hailey house. The long front yard was packed with vehicles, children playing, and parents sitting under trees. Harry Rex parked and a crowd rushed to greet Carl Lee's lawyer. Lester held him and said, "You've done it again!"

Carl Lee came out and they shook hands and smiled at each other, both searching for words. They put their arms round each other. The crowd clapped and shouted.

"Thank you, Jake," Carl Lee said softly.

◆

At two-thirty, Jake sat at his desk and talked to Carla on the phone, while Lucien and Harry Rex drank beer. He told his wife he would leave in three hours and be in North Carolina tomorrow. Yes, he was fine, he said. Everything was OK. It was all finished. There was a crowd of reporters in his conference room, so she shouldn't miss the evening news. He said he loved her.

Tomorrow, he'd call Ellen.

"Why are you leaving?" Lucien demanded.

"You're stupid, Jake, just stupid," Harry Rex shouted. "You've got a thousand reporters waiting for you and you're leaving town. Stupid, just stupid."

Jake stood up. "How do I look?"

"Pretty stupid if you leave," Harry Rex said.

"Wait for a couple of days," Lucien said. "This is an opportunity you'll never have again. Please, Jake."

"Relax. I'm going to meet them now, let them take my picture, answer a few questions. Then I'm leaving town. I've got to talk to my wife. I've got a lot of explaining to do."

"You're crazy, Jake," Harry Rex said.

"I agree!" said Lucien.

Jake looked in the mirror, straightened his borrowed tie, and smiled at his friends.

"I love you two. I really do. And hey! I got paid nine hundred dollars for this trial, and I plan to share it with you."

They emptied the last cans of beer and followed Jake Brigance down the stairs to face the reporters.

ACTIVITIES

Chapters 1–3

Before you read

1 This book is called *A Time to Kill*. Do you think there are any situations in which it is acceptable to kill someone? What are they?

2 Use your dictionary to check the meanings of these words. The words are all in the story.

arrest case client county defendant deputy insane mask nigger nod pickup prosecute psychiatrist publicize rape robe whiskey

    a Which are words for people? Which word is very offensive? Which person might examine someone who is *insane*?

    b Which are words for actions? Which action is a crime?

    c Which are words for clothes? Who wears clothes like these?

    d Which is a word for a vehicle? What kind of vehicle?

    e Which is a word for a drink? What other alcoholic drinks can you name?

    f Which is a word for a part of a state? How is your country divided?

    g What is a legal *case*? How does it end?

3 The word *ain't* is common in American speech. It is a negative short form of the verbs *be* or *have*. Write the full forms of these statements:

    a "I ain't moving."

    b "White people ain't got a chance."

After you read

4 Who says these words? Who or what are they talking about?

    a "Let's throw her off a bridge."

    b "Are you ready to defend another member of my family?"

    c "You'd better come with me."

    d "You charged Lester five thousand."

    e "Congratulations."

5 Discuss adjectives to describe these characters:

  a Jake Brigance   **c** Ozzie Clark

  b Carl Lee Hailey   **d** Lucien Wilbanks

Chapters 4–6

Before you read

6 In your country, what happens to someone after they have been arrested? List the stages of the legal process. Compare them with the process in the United States as you continue reading.

7 Answer these questions. Check the meanings of the words in *italics*.

  a If a person or decision is *reasonable*, is it fair?

  b What kind of building would you look in to find someone with the title *Reverend*?

After you read

8 Who are these people? Why are they important to the story?

  a Rufus Buckley   **e** Noose

  b Stump Sisson   **f** Ollie Agee

  c Freddie Cobb   **g** Dr. W.T. Bass

  d Harry Rex Vonner

9 In your country, is it possible to use insanity as a defense in a murder trial? Discuss whether it *should* be a possible defense.

Chapters 7–9

Before you read

10 What is the attitude of people to female lawyers in your country? Is it the same as their attitude to male lawyers?

11 Look up these words in your dictionary. Then complete the following paragraph with forms of the words.

dynamite porch qualification research select tick

Henry had a low-paid job and wanted to find a better one. One evening he was sitting on the ….. reading about some recent ….. into the kinds of ….. that help people to be ….. for top jobs. Conscious of a ….. noise under his chair, he looked down and saw a clock connected to a stick of .... He had never run so fast in his life!

After you read

12 Answer these questions.
  a Why is Jake's assistant, Ethel, worried about money?
  b Why does Ozzie wake Jake in the middle of the night?
  c Why is Jake's wife, Carla, not speaking to him?
  d Why does Jake accept Ellen's offer of help?
  e What happens to Bud Twitty?
  f How does Ozzie persuade Reverend Agee to produce the money that was collected for Carl Lee?
13 Why does Ellen Roark want to help Jake Brigance? List the reasons that you think are most important to her.

Chapters 10–12

Before you read

14 If you had to help Jake Brigance choose the jury for Carl Lee Hailey's trial, what kind of jury do you think would give Carl Lee the fairest trial? Why?
  a mostly black males   **d** mostly white females
  b mostly black females   **e** another combination
  c mostly white males
15 Answer these questions. Check the meanings of the words in *italics*.
  a If you are *charged* with a crime, do the police believe that you are guilty or innocent?
  b Which two of these people probably use the word *evidence* most frequently in their job?
      a police officer   a baker   a lawyer   a teacher   a builder
  c If a lawyer objects to another lawyer's statement in court, and the judge says "*Sustained,*" does the judge agree or disagree with the objection?
  d Are people more likely to feel hatred or pity for the *victim* of a crime?

After you read

16 In what ways does Deputy Looney's evidence help Carl Lee?

17 Three terrible things happen to Jake and Ellen in this section of the book. What are they?

Chapters 13–14

Before you read

18 How will the trial end, do you think? What will Jake do when it ends?

After you read

19 How many defendants has Dr. Rodeheaver seen who he did not think were insane? Why does Jake think that this is important?

20 Discuss how and why Wanda Wornack is able to persuade the rest of the jury to reach a decision.

Writing

21 Jake Brigance is a lawyer, but he understands when Carl Lee kills the two rapists. How do you feel about Carl Lee's actions? Discuss the reasons for and against your views.

22 Sheriff Ozzie Clark uses violence when he arrests some of the people in this story. Should the police use this kind of force? Give reasons for your opinion.

23 You are reporting on the Carl Lee Hailey case for a New York paper. Write a short article reporting the jury's decision.

24 Write the conversation between Jake Brigance and his wife Carla when they meet again at her parents' house.

25 "Rape is the worst crime of violence." Do you agree or disagree with this statement? Give your reasons.

26 Imagine you are Ellen Roark. Write a letter to Jake a month after leaving hospital. Tell him what you are feeling, what you are doing now, and your plans for the future.